# Coming home

## A Mormon's Return to Faith

Susan N. Swann

New Voices
B O O K S

Coming Home:
A Mormon's Return to Faith

Copyright © New Voices Books, 2011

ISBN: 978-0-9848645-0-8

New Voices Books

E-mail: newvoicesbooks@hotmail.com

Visit the author at: http://www.returntofaith.org

Printed in the United States of America.

# CONTENTS

# PROLOGUE

In my wildest dreams, I could never once have imagined leaving the Mormon Church. I'd been a member all my life. My ancestors crossed the plains. They were with Joseph Smith in the beginning. They left behind all they had for the Church—more than once. My dad was a bishop. All three of my brothers had been bishops. I'd been a relief society president. I thought I'd built my house upon the rock. But when the real storms came, my house of faith crumbled to liquefied sand.

I can't fully explain why hardship drove me away from my faith, while others around me who also experienced trials held fast. I do know that unanticipated pain and loss led me to ask "Why me?" or "Why them and why not me?" Bitterness and resentment over unexpected turns and twists in my life festered and morphed into an unbelief that did not serve me well in the end. I would be gone for almost 15 years before I came back.

I was fortunate that family members and friends remained beside me. They refused to let go of me or give up on me. No matter how stubborn or difficult or blind or unrepentant I was, no matter how long it took, they held fast until I made room in my heart for the Lord to soften my feelings and wrench my heart strings until, similar to the prodigal son, I "came to myself," and found my way home.

My purpose in sharing my story is a simple attempt to reach out to those who may also be struggling, or to those with family members who may be struggling. It's meant ultimately to be a message of hope, gratitude, and love. It's filled with people who held on to me as I struggled for years to get my bearings. This was neither a quick nor painless process for those who loved me. I'd like to think it was worth it in the end.

# PART I

# LOST IN THE MIST

*And it came to pass that there arose a mist of darkness;
yea, even an exceedingly great mist of darkness,
insomuch that they who had commenced in the path did
lose their way, that they wandered off and were lost.*

—I NEPHI 8:23

# I

# Orange County, California

*S*outh Orange County nestles up against sparkling, blue waters. It's a place possessed by sun-drenched beaches, kissed by cool ocean breezes. It's the advertised location of the happiest place on earth. But for me, at that time and in that place, the world that I had so carefully crafted was crumbling around me. My life was coming apart in my hands. It didn't look at all like what I had planned for or expected.

Somewhere along the way, I think I had somehow come to believe that if I just did everything right, nothing would ever go wrong. This has never been true, of course—not for anyone. I understood the fallacy of this kind of thinking deep in the recesses of my mind, but emotionally I held fast to the magical belief that "right makes might," such that if I did everything right, I might expect to be shielded from life's problems. That didn't turn out to be the case.

My marriage of 20 years had begun to fray. It's difficult to pinpoint the exact reason. Some of it was me. Some of it was him. Some of it was the result of ongoing financial losses that first swamped and eventually overwhelmed us. The end of the line for me came one day in June of 1995.

I had no idea just how bad things were about to get when I pulled up outside the bank and ran my card through the ATM. I keyed in a withdrawal of $100. Nothing came out. The screen said there was no money in my account. That is simply not possible, I thought. In disbelief, I tried again. Still nothing. I rolled up the window, pulled forward out of the drive-through, and drove around to the front door. I got out of my car, pushed through the double-glass doors, and hurried up to the nearest teller.

"There's been some kind of mistake," I told the woman with the sun-streaked hair and warm smile, sitting behind the desk. "I deposited my student loan check into my account several days ago for more than two thousand dollars. But my balance shows as zero."

"Hmmmm . . ." she responded, firing up her computer, fake nails clacking on the keys. "Let me check." As my account came up on her screen, her warm smile disappeared. She looked at me suspiciously.

"There's been no mistake," she pronounced coldly. "The IRS seized the money in your account."

"The *who?*" I asked incredulously.

"The IRS," she whispered, leaning across the desk.

"Can they do that?"

"They can . . . and they did."

"Is there anything I can do?" I asked her, gripping the arms of my chair. "I didn't know anything about this!"

"I'm afraid you'll have to take that up with the IRS," she said, a bit more sympathetically. "I'm sorry."

I stumbled out of the bank and somehow found my way to the car. This couldn't be. I needed this money to pay my graduate school tuition and buy the week's groceries. I knew we had no money. The Church had even been paying our rent for the past few months. But was it also possible that we hadn't been paying our taxes?

I sat in my car stunned. My stomach knotted. Whenever anything gets particularly bad, my stomach knots. Finally the stuff that was knotting my stomach bubbled over. Rivers of tears ran down my face and splashed onto my jeans. I felt lost and utterly alone. How did I ever get here? This wasn't how my life was supposed to turn out.

I knew we were struggling financially, but I didn't know we were in trouble with the IRS. And I was pretty sure I couldn't take the roller coaster ride anymore. We were up, we were down. We had money, we had none. We bought homes, we lost them. Three times. And now even my student loan money was gone.

My tears stopped as suddenly as they started. I looked down at my slightly soggy jeans, and my sadness turned to anger. I threw my car into gear and sped home. I was livid. As I approached the house, I remember being relieved that my 12-year old son and 17-year old daughter were still at school.

I walked through the front door and saw a letter sitting open on our glass coffee table in the living room. It was from the IRS, demanding payment for back taxes. The letter outlined their intent to seize our bank accounts, which by now they already had. I stood there for a moment and just gazed around the room. Incredibly, it looked the same as it had earlier that day. My son's basketball was still sitting in the corner. Towels I had folded that morning were still waiting to be put in the linen closet. It all looked so normal.

I went into the family room, picked up the phone, and called the IRS. After waiting on hold for about 30 minutes, I finally got a voice on the other end. "IRS. How can I help you?"

"I'm calling about a letter we got in the mail. My bank account was levied. My student loan money is gone."

"May I have your social security number, please?"

I gave it to him. While he was looking, I asked him if there was anything I could do to get my student loan money back.

"I'm afraid, not," he answered. You're behind in making payments on back taxes."

"I didn't know that," I answered.

"You didn't know about the back taxes?" he asked skeptically.

"I knew about the back taxes. I just didn't know my husband wasn't making payments. Is there anything we can do to renew our payment arrangements?"

"That depends. I see that you haven't yet filed your taxes for this year. It looks as if you filed an extension."

"That's true," I said. I knew about that too.

"Do you owe any taxes for this year?"

"I don't know," I answered truthfully. "My husband pays our bills and taxes through his business account." The sinking feeling in my stomach yawned into an open pit.

"I'm afraid I can't make payment arrangements until we know about your taxes for 1994."

"I'll get back to you," I said to the agent, and hung up the phone.

I angrily confronted my husband about our taxes for 1994. And then I asked him if we owed any money. His response to me was "probably." When I asked him how much we'd paid in taxes for all of 1994, his answer was, "nothing." In my head, one domino fell, pushed on another, and another, until all the dominoes were down. How could I have been so blind?

I was so furious I could barely speak. And then I said simply, "I'm leaving you."

As I uttered those words, they didn't even sound like me. I had no idea where I would go or what I would do. This certainly wasn't the first problem we'd had in our marriage—but I was pretty sure it would be the last. We didn't seem to be able to find ways to work together anymore on anything that mattered.

We tried marriage counseling. People have to be willing to change for counseling to work. We weren't. It didn't help that even prior to our most recent problems, I'd begun questioning my faith. Over and over, I found myself asking—to no one in particular—the most useless of all questions. Why me?

It also didn't help that I looked for and found support outside my marriage. Looking back, I think that's when things really started slipping away from me. The loss of the Spirit was gradual, but sure. It was so slow that it was almost imperceptible. I could barely sense that my spiritual eyes were closing. But as my thinking changed, and my perspective shifted, I drifted further away.

Three weeks after the IRS seized my bank account, I took my children and moved out. Some of my reasons for leaving are too personal for these pages. The financial train wreck certainly wasn't the only thing that toppled our temple marriage. But for my part, I had finally hit a wall. This time there was no going back. My children cried. I cried. My husband cried. But in the end, I ended it and took my children with me.

We left with nothing: we had no place to live; I had no car and no job. And I was in trouble with the IRS. I looked for a tax agent to represent me. I found a woman in the yellow pages. Her picture was posted in her advertisement for tax services. She seemed to gaze out at me from the pages of the phone book with what looked like kind eyes. I wanted a woman to help me, and there weren't that many women I could find who were enrolled agents with the Department of the Treasury. So I called Marilyn.

Marilyn did the best she could, but ultimately the IRS refused my offer in compromise, not believing that I was an "innocent spouse." So I made payments to them until I could legally take out bankruptcy to discharge the back taxes. The interest and penalties were mounting so fast, I figured it would take me more than twenty years to dig myself out of the hole.

The day I went before the judge to declare bankruptcy was worse for me than the day my divorce was final. I was so ashamed. I never, ever, wanted to see the dress again that I'd worn during the bankruptcy proceedings. Regardless of how little money I had, I took that dress out to the dumpster, tossed it to the bottom of the trash, and snapped the lid closed. That was the day I hit bottom financially. I had not yet hit bottom spiritually.

## II

# Leaving the Saints

*"Yet hath he not root in himself . . .*
*by and by he is offended." —Matthew 13:21*

*M*y situation grew darker. As my foundation crumbled underneath me, I began revisiting decisions I'd made over the past 20 years. I found myself wondering about choices I thought had been inspired. Events in my life that I had counted as blessings suddenly didn't seem that way anymore. As my fear and anger grew, my faith waned. I could find no forgiveness in my heart for those I thought had hurt and wronged me. My bitterness over life's losses became a poison that soon infected my own well.

I became increasingly disillusioned. My world no longer made sense to me. I began to ask, where is God? Why did he allow this to happen to me and my family? I've always tried to be a good person. Tried to do everything right. How could I find myself here? When no good answers came, my faith cracked and shattered into bits of broken glass.

I pulled away from those who wanted to help. I no longer felt comfortable at church. It wasn't long before I had no desire to return. I came to rely on reason and lost all faith. Spiritual things became foolish to me. I stopped believing that there was anything out there "bigger" than I was and began to believe not in God, but in the ultimate randomness of life's events.

Since I couldn't find a way to resolve the questions I had, I continued the process of dismantling my beliefs. I decided that I might be better off relying on my own decisions, rather than following what I had thought were spiritual promptings. A wall of doubt began to separate me from what I once believed and loved most.

This didn't happen all at once. But little by little, as doubts and fears went unchecked, I veered off the path I had followed all my life. I was now no longer living my life in harmony with the teachings of my church. I felt guilty and confused. I wandered deeper into the mist of darkness. I let go of the iron rod and listened to the mocking voices of those who did not believe in God or the Church.

The Church continued to try and help me and my children. They offered food. I had food, but my money was stretched pretty thin. So I accepted the offer of one food order from the Bishop's storehouse. Not long before, I had helped other families get food orders. And now I was getting one myself. I had always believed that it was my job to help others. Not that it was other people's jobs to help me. I could not humble myself and accept help.

On one of the Sundays when I was still sporadically attending church, Bishop Reese caught up with me in the hall. "How are you doing, Susan," he asked solicitously. "What can I do for you?" I'd always loved Curtis Reese. And I knew he was trying to help me. He was also a man of integrity with a deep and abiding faith, and I admired that about him.

"I'm ok, Curtis. Thanks," I answered more bravely than I felt. "I've got it covered."

"That's good. And what about your faith? Do you think you can find a way to believe in the Church again?" I resisted his concern.

"I don't even believe in God anymore, Curtis. Let alone the Church."

Then he said, "Susan, if you can't believe in God or Christ, just believe Christ. Believe in what he taught." It was an interesting idea, I had to admit, but my spiritual ears were closed to all things of a spiritual nature.

"I don't think I can do that, Bishop," I replied.

So he just hugged me, told me he loved me, and predicted that one day I'd come back. "I don't think so, Curtis," I replied. "I'm never coming back." Then he asked me a question whose logic I could not refute.

"Let me ask you this, Susan," he said. "When you were active in the Church, could you ever have imagined a time when you would have left?"

"No Bishop," I responded softly. "I never would have thought I would ever leave."

"Then how can you dismiss the possibility that one day you might come back?" He had me there. I had no good come back. So I just smiled, shook my head, and walked away.

I began reading more opposing points of view about LDS history and culture. Since I couldn't see myself leaving the Church over the behavior of others, I looked for ways to discredit the doctrine. There's no shortage of critical literature out there, so materials were easy to come by. It wasn't long before I lost both my footing and my testimony altogether. Eventually, I removed my garments. I broke my temple covenants. I abandoned my traditions and took my two children with me.

I stopped believing in both the Church and in God. I decided that religion was for the weak minded. The light fled, and I could not see at all through the darkness. All this happened before my extended family fully realized what was taking place. They sensed that I was struggling spiritually. But they didn't know until later just how much. The day I finally told my mother I was no longer a believer was a particularly painful one for both of us.

I found more friends and associates outside my faith. New companions who reframed my decision to leave the Church as courageous. I had escaped, they told me. Others celebrated the end of my marriage, rather than grieving it. Always there were those who helped me "look through my own glass darkly."

My family was in shock for a long time. My divorce was one thing; leaving the Church was quite another. Who was I now anyway, they wondered? What could they expect from me? We struggled to redefine our relationships without our deep-rooted beliefs to connect us. It was hard. My nieces and nephews, whom I adored, were the most confused. My mom especially wrestled with the idea that she had somehow failed me. But in or out of the Church, my family loved me still. And on most days, I knew it.

I was not yet as Job. I still had my family, friends, my health and my children. But this was not a time when I found myself counting my blessings. Job found strength by placing his trust in the Lord. He maintained his integrity. Rather than enduring my trials with faithfulness, I chose to "curse God" for my misfortune and press forward alone, struggling daily just to put one foot in front of the other.

By this time, my daughter insisted on moving to Utah to finish her last year of high school, while my son stayed with me. She'd had enough. What was left for her in California? Reluctantly, I agreed with my husband to let her go to Utah. We were a fragmented and fractured little family with as yet no visible means of support. I felt as though I were such an incredible failure.

# III

# My Journey Begins

*"... Let all these take their journey unto one place,*
*in their several courses, and one man shall not build upon*
*another's foundation, neither journey in another's track."*
—D&C 52:33

One particularly dark day, I sobbed on the phone to my mom that I had lost my marriage and no longer had a family. "You still have a family, Susan," she asserted firmly. "You have a mother, three brothers, sisters-in-law, 2 children, and 14 nieces and nephews who adore you. You have always been, and will always be, part of this family. You will forever have us." Her words made me cry.

At this point, most of all, I needed to find a way to regain my financial footing. After borrowing a car for six weeks from my friend Renee, I walked in to the local Ford dealership one bright day in August to try and buy a car with no money down, no credit, and no job. I convinced myself to think positively. I assured the salesman working with me that I was completing a master's degree and would find a way to get back on my feet. After a few hours of back and forth, his boss decided I might be worth the risk and agreed to lease me a shiny, new, green Ford Aspire. The interest rate was astronomical, but the car was mine.

When my son Alex saw it, he told me it looked like a wind-up toy. I laughed and admitted that it did. I told him we were broke, and times were tough. He refused to accept that way of looking at things and said,

"No Mom. We're just financially challenged." I loved him for saying that. I knew he had faith in me to make things better. I hoped he was right.

We had our own transportation again, and by now a small 2-bedroom apartment to call home. I was grateful to my mom who gave me the first 3 months rent, and to Renee, who co-signed with me for the first 6 months of the lease.

I was soon working both in and out of the home and finishing my degree. I taught an adult night class. I wrote reading passages and test questions for a publisher. I had just one year of my master's program to go. Alex wanted to help me in whatever way he could. And doing his own laundry was one of the ways he did that.

I watched him one day out of our 3-story apartment window load his big laundry basket onto his skateboard and skate his own clothes across the parking lot to our on-site laundry facility. It broke my heart to watch him struggle with the load, but I knew he didn't want my help. My eyes welled with tears of pride in my young son.

A year later, after I graduated and found a job, we could finally afford to buy a washer and dryer. Alex came with me to pick them out. He was thrilled to be getting a new washer and dryer and anxious to make the purchase. He ran happily from one set of machines to another, reading me the list of options. An older couple walking by us in the store commented to me that they had never seen a boy so excited about buying a washer and dryer. I just smiled, thinking about the year-long, weekly trips Alex had made across the parking lot with his laundry.

We bought the bottom of the line models, but Alex made sure that they had all-temperature wash and dry cycles. They worked beautifully for years. More importantly, there would be no more skateboarding trips with laundry in tow. Alex was so happy; he spent the entire afternoon washing everything he could find in the house—even my sheets and towels.

The Church continued to try and help us, when I'd let them. Which wasn't often. I was filled with an intense desire to make it on my own. And while I had soundly rejected my community of faith, they waited patiently, ever watchful, hoping one day that I would come back.

I didn't think much at all about coming back, until one warm spring evening, one of my Pepperdine psychology professors brought my feelings about the Church into sharp focus. The topic of our class discussion was the role that the beliefs and traditions of our families play in our lives. I was fascinated by a story he related to highlight his point. As I remember it, the story was about a man who grew up in a remote village.

This man had given up the beliefs and traditions of his family and his village years ago. He had decided they were just superstition—until one day, word came from the village elders that a neighboring village was preparing to attack. He considered calling on the family spirits for protection. That was silly, he reasoned. But whether or not it was silly suddenly didn't matter to him. He was afraid, and he needed help. He prayed for protection.

As my professor ended his story, the class discussed the pull of family values and religious traditions. I thought about how the man in the village, after abandoning his former ways of doing things, turned to them again. Intellectually it made no sense to him: but emotionally and spiritually it did.

Similar to the man in the story, I didn't really believe in things spiritual anymore. But the story intrigued me and made me wonder if religion might possibly ever again play a role in my life. I spent half an hour after class talking with my professor about the painful rejection of beliefs I had held all my life. He listened carefully and then in so many words said: "Susan, all your life you have held a set of beliefs. It was your thesis for living life. In rejecting those beliefs, what you have now is not so much a new set of beliefs, as an antithesis of what you have believed up to this point. Over time, you will find a way to synthesize your beliefs into a new whole. I don't know whether or not you will find your synthesis in the faith you've left, or somewhere else. But you will find it."

His words hit me hard and made me realize that I was still very angry with the Church. I was angry that I had followed what I viewed as divine direction in my life, only to find myself on a serious detour in my life's journey. I realized as I listened to my professor, however, that merely being against something did not constitute being for something else.

I thought about times I had seen anti-Mormon protestors outside the Salt Lake temple. I knew that some of them were former Mormons who no longer believed. Some of them were so angry with the Church that they went so far as to chain themselves to the gates of the temple in protest. These people, to my way of thinking, didn't know what they believed: they only knew what they didn't believe. The absence of belief, as far as I was concerned, did not constitute a belief in something else.

So I decided to quit worrying about what I no longer believed and search instead for what I could believe. I made an uneasy peace with the Church and stopped being angry. I viewed the Church's beliefs with the same respect that I accorded the beliefs of all other religions, and I began my own search for answers. I was pretty much starting from scratch, which was a disconcerting place to be. I hoped that at some point, I would reach the place of synthesis my professor described.

That night was the beginning of a long struggle for me. It was a struggle that was invisible to my family and friends in the Church. Much of the time, it was invisible even to me.

As I began my journey to some, as yet, unspecified destination, I didn't know that "the end of all [my] exploring would be to arrive where [I] started and know the place for the first time." (T. S. Eliot)

# IV

# Graduation at Last

*"And Thou Hast Strengthened the Feeble Knees." —Job 4:4*

As I prepared for graduation from Pepperdine in June of 1996, I had to admit that I hadn't always been sure this day would ever come. There were others who weren't so sure either. When things went south financially, there were some who suggested that I give up, or at the very least postpone, getting my master's degree and look for work as a teacher instead. I had my California credential. So that was a possibility.

But I was convinced that education was never wasted and that I had a brighter future ahead of me with a master's degree. My dream was to finish collecting the required clinical hours and get my license as a therapist. I wanted to open my own practice. Go to work for myself. So I pressed on, piling up more student debt as I went.

I'd been working part time for a small company as an independent contractor writing reading passages and test questions, which was at least putting food on the table. I was surprised when they offered me a full-time job, several months prior to my June graduation.

When they brought me in for an interview, I told the VP who interviewed me that my dream was to be a therapist. She certainly understood that, she said. She also knew that financial reality was smacking me squarely in the face, and that I needed a full time job. Yesterday wouldn't be too soon.

"Maybe you can build new dreams in the education industry," she offered. "You can start by working 30 hours a week until you graduate, and then we'll bring you on full time." It was a generous offer. And the job came with health benefits, which Alex and I sorely needed.

The salary she offered me was about what I could make as a beginning therapist, and I wouldn't have to collect 3,000 clinical hours before I began work. The job required a master's degree, which I'd almost completed. She dangled the promise of regular pay raises and promotions.

It was too good to pass up. So I decided to give up my dream of becoming a therapist, which is what I'd trained to do for years. And I loved the work. That particular dream died very hard for me. At the time, I saw it as just one more of my life's dreams gone up in smoke.

But with June now approaching, I just wanted to graduate and move on with my life. I'd been working more than fifty hours a week outside our home for the past 6 months. Alex was still just 13, and I hated being away from him that much. It wasn't fair to him. I also felt as though it was time to quit relying on the kindness of several friends, who let Alex spend week nights in their homes, until I could come to pick him up.

My mother and my three brothers were aware that I was getting ready to graduate. They knew how hard I'd worked. They each told me that there was no way they were going to miss being there. Norm would drive the few hours it would take to get to Malibu from Glendora. Brent, Dave, and my mom would fly in together.

I was excited that the commencement exercises would be held at the Malibu campus, which sits cradled in the foothills of the Santa Monica Mountains. To my way of thinking, it is one of the most beautiful locations for a college campus anywhere in the world, with its rolling green hills and commanding view of the Pacific Ocean. I'd been on the Malibu campus a few times before, and I loved the scenic drive up Pacific Coast Highway along the rugged Malibu coastline. It was absolutely breathtaking.

The convocation was scheduled to start promptly at 10:00 a.m. All graduates were required to be on campus at least one hour prior to start time to pick up caps and gowns and line up for the processional, which meant we'd have to leave home early to get there in time. "Let's go, Alex," I called that morning, grabbing my hood.

"Right behind you, Mom," Alex said, stopping to pick up the camera.

I was happy when we passed through the Los Angeles smog and turned onto Pacific Coast Highway. We rolled down our windows so we could inhale the fresh, clean air. The marine layer was just starting to lift. I could see the sun fighting its way through the overcast sky. It was going to be a beautiful day in Malibu.

We drove onto the Pepperdine Campus and parked the car. Alex went to save seats, while I went to put on my cap and gown. My mom had helped me buy a new dress for the occasion. I still remember how much I liked that straight, black sheath with its black and tan vertically striped overlay. I donned my black robe and placed the blue and orange hood over my head and around my shoulders. I added the gold cord with gold and blue tassels and walked over to the growing line of graduates.

I stood talking with friends I'd made over the past two years, knowing that I'd never see some of them again. It was a bittersweet moment, as graduations always are for me. We soon walked single file down the hill and readied to make our grand entrance. Alex came running up and placed a lovely bouquet of red and yellow flowers in my arms. One of my brothers must have helped him buy it, I thought. He flashed me a big smile. "I'm really proud of you, Mom," he said, quickly taking my picture before he ran off to join the others.

As we neared the entrance, the orchestra began playing "Pomp and Circumstance." That did it for me. I'm just one of those people who always cry when I hear that song. So many graduations. So many endings. So many new beginnings.

When I finally walked in, my family clapped. Alex clapped the loudest and shouted, "Go, Mom!" We took our seats.

I must admit I don't really remember much about what the commencement speaker said that day. I'm sure he delivered an inspirational message. I think it was something about the importance of an education and how an education should lead to a life of service. I was so caught up in a life of survival that a life of service was not really on my agenda at the moment.

The time finally arrived for the dean of our college to present us with our diplomas. As I walked across the stage to receive my diploma, my family again rose to their feet and cheered. Once again my Alex whistled and cheered the loudest.

As we gathered afterward on the lawn, my family each hugged me in turn and handed me graduation cards. My mother's card particularly moved me. Her words read: "Dear Susan, You are to be greatly admired. You have worked hard to conquer the turmoil and problems in your life. At the same time, you have achieved your academic goal. I am so very proud of you." I wept openly when I read her words again at the end of the evening in the privacy of my bedroom.

My mom took us all out for a late lunch at Gladstone's restaurant following graduation. We ate seafood and celebrated. We looked out at the ocean and watched the sailboats pass by. We talked and we laughed. We munched peanuts and threw our shells on the floor, along with the rest of the patrons. Alex particularly liked that part.

When we finally got home, I found another graduation card in my mailbox. This one was from Bishop Reese. On the bottom he wrote: "Congratulations and keep smiling. Love, Curtis." He included a scripture reference from the Book of Mormon: 2 Nephi 5: 27. I looked it up. It read: "And it came to pass that we lived after the manner of happiness."

As I thought about it, I wasn't even sure what the manner of happiness was anymore. I was still wandering around in the mist. Not only did I see no way out, I didn't even know I had gotten lost. That would come later. Much later.

# PART 2

# TENDER MERCIES

*Let thy tender mercies come unto me, that I may live.*

—PSALM 119:77

# V

# Highway 57 North

Once my 3 younger brothers had fully taken stock of my situation, Brent and Dave thought Alex and I should move closer to one of them. Brent knew I was taking mediation courses in my master's program. He was an attorney in Twin Falls, and he thought he might be able to send some business my way. My mother also lived in Twin, so it was kind of natural to think that it might be a good idea for us to move there.

Dave knew that I still had friends who lived in Salt Lake. Perhaps I'd like to move there? My brother Norm didn't need to ask me to move closer to him . . . he already lived just about 50 miles away from me in Glendora.

What to do? I still had some kind of life in Laguna Niguel. Alex didn't want to leave his friends, and neither did I. And somehow it made me feel defeated to think that I couldn't bloom where I was planted. I loved living in California. So, for better or worse, Alex and I stayed put. And for the next 9 years, until they moved to Salt Lake, Norm and his family were our family in residence.

Norm was the closest to me in age. Growing up, I'd been the "big sister example" to all three of my brothers, just as my dad had admonished me to be. "Your brothers look up to you, Susan," he said. "Always do the right thing and be an example to them."

I'd tried to do that pretty much all my life. I loved my brothers, cared for them, and protected them. As we grew up together in our small, rural Idaho town, kids in our neighborhood and schools knew they had better not mess with my little brothers. Or they'd have to answer to me. If I weren't big enough or strong enough to protect them, I'd find someone who was—or I'd go get my dad.

Because I'd grown up with 3 brothers and no sisters, I learned quickly how important it was to keep up with boys. How could I be a proper big sister if I were afraid to do the things they did? So if one of them jumped out of the tree house in our backyard into a big bank of soft, white snow, I felt I had to do the same. If one of them jumped off of lava rocks into hot springs below, I followed suit, even when the "cliffs" seemed high, and I was secretly afraid. When they threw out the challenge of the dreaded "double-dog dare," I simply felt compelled to comply.

Another imperative my dad issued was that we each represent our family well. "You're a Nielson," he proclaimed regularly. "Nielsons don't wear jeans to high school. Nielsons don't go downtown in grubby clothes. Nielsons get good grades. Nielsons achieve. Nielsons watch out for each other. Remember that your name, your reputation, and your family are your most valuable assets."

And now here I was divorced, broke, and inactive. I was no longer an example to my brothers. I no longer had standing in any community. I didn't even have the same name I grew up with. I was the quintessential black sheep. It was a good thing my dad hadn't lived to see all of this, I thought.

I learned later that one of my family members thought I needed a family intervention over my inactivity in the Church. The idea was that they would all sit me down and let me know how strongly they felt about my leaving the Church. It was my brother Norm who wisely advised against that particular action. However well-intended it might have been, I was far too fragile to have responded to confrontation, and what I would have perceived as judgment and rejection. It would have only served to drive me further away from them.

And so it was Norm who ended up living closest to me. It was Norm who advised love and patience regarding my inactivity in the Church. It was Norm who held most tightly to the back of my jacket, so I would not slip away into the mist forever.

October was approaching, and my birthday was coming up. I wasn't looking forward to it, which was unusual for me. Whether they were mine or someone else's, birthdays had always been a big deal. Prior to now, when it came to birthdays, my motto had always been, "Anything worth doing is worth over doing." This year I didn't want to "do" a birthday at all. I could think of nothing to celebrate. Maybe I could just skip this year. Pretend it never, *ever* happened.

Then I got a call from Norm. "Hi, Susan."

"Hey, Norm."

"How about coming over to our house for a birthday dinner?"

"Thanks, Norm. That's nice. I don't think I'd be particularly good company this year."

"You don't have to be good company, Susan. Just come and spend the day with us. We're making your favorite birthday dinner. You won't want to miss it. "

"You're cooking turkey with all the trimmings?" I asked.

"Absolutely. And German chocolate cake made from scratch. And Karla's homemade rolls. What do you say?" It was thoughtful of Norm to not only remember what my favorite birthday dinner was, but to also offer to make it for me.

"Sounds tempting," I said. "But I don't know. Maybe I should just hang out here."

"And do what?" Norm asked. "And what about Alex? He'll want to celebrate your birthday."

Alex had been pretty down the past few months, just as I had. And who could blame him? I'd just broken up his family. I still sometimes found him sitting alone in his room, just playing with his old Legos that he hadn't touched in years. Norm was right. It would do us both good to get out of the house and spend the day with family.

"Ok, Norm. You're right. We'll come . . . And thank you for thinking of us."

"Excellent! Come early. Say about noon? Or come anytime you want."

"Sure. We can be there by then. See you soon."

The day came to drive to Glendora. I'd already opened Alex's cute birthday card. He'd included handmade certificates good for helping me around the house. I hugged him gratefully. He was happy that we were going to his cousins' house for dinner and birthday cake. He didn't want me to go without a cake.

We left the apartment that morning in our little green Ford Aspire. We turned up the radio loudly and found one of Alex's favorite stations on the dial, so that Alex could "bump some tunes," as he used to like to say. We pulled onto the freeway and followed the signs to Highway 57 North to Glendora. About an hour later, we exited onto Auto Center Drive and turned right. We were almost there.

When we pulled up out front, the kids tumbled out the door to greet us. Lots of hugs, smiles and "welcomes." As we sat down to eat, Norm and I talked and laughed and regaled the kids with stories about growing up in Burley. Karla and I discussed the books we were reading. We all played family games together. I loved being with my nieces and nephews. They were fun, talkative, and conversant on most topics. They laughed and teased both each other and Alex and me.

On another Sunday when Alex and I were in Glendora for dinner, Norm's home teacher dropped by for a visit. His name was Carl Fonoimoana. He was Samoan. He was a strong, kind, polished man. He was also gentle and well spoken. Alex was impressed with him and his outsized spirit. He listened closely to what he said.

Brother Fonoimoana spoke to Alex about the importance and power of mothers. He looked right at Alex and told him in no uncertain terms: "Respect your mother, Alex. Always have a great respect for her. She watches out for you." I watched Alex nod in rapt agreement. I felt something powerful listening to Brother Fonoimoana. And so did Alex. We talked about it on the way home. I'm sure I didn't identify what I felt as the Spirit. The Spirit had to shout very loudly at that point for me to hear anything at all.

Brother Fonoimoana helped both me and my son that night in Glendora. I'm sure he's helped so many people, he doesn't even remember the night he helped us. He's the kind of person who just sees a need and fills it.

Alex and I would make the drive up Highway 57 North to Glendora countless times over the next 9 years. We went annually for my favorite birthday dinner, we went for Easter, we went for many Christmas Eves, and summer cook outs. We were always welcome in, and invited to, Norm's home. My brother Norm and his family were a collective light that often illuminated the dark corners of my life.

*"Neither do men light a candle, and put it under a bushel, but on a candlestick; and it giveth light to all that are in the house."* Matthew 5: 15

# VI

## All Her Fingers and Toes

*J*t was a cold, wintry day in February of 1997 when Alex and I boarded the silver plane to Utah. I was going to be with my baby girl while she gave birth to her baby girl. At not quite 19, my daughter was still just a child herself.

I sat on the plane staring blankly at the heads of the passengers in front of me. I was angry—mostly with myself for not finding a way to keep Alicia with me after the divorce. What kind of mother lets her 17-year old daughter move to Utah on her own? I wondered how her life might have been different if I'd insisted on keeping her with me. Unanswerable questions that wouldn't change anything now, I thought, as the plane winged its way across the gray and orange sky.

I turned my head to the window to hide the tears of sadness, regret, and pain that I could feel starting to run down my face. My daughter was so young to be a mother. She had no husband and no job. She wouldn't even be graduating from high school until spring. Her life would be forever altered. This was not the way I had wanted things to work for her.

I was doing my best to keep it together when the flight attendant handed me a napkin and kindly asked me what I wanted to drink. "Water, no ice, please," I said, trying not to look up at her. As I sat sipping my water, I briefly allowed myself to speculate on the possibility that if I'd stayed active in church, perhaps the events of the past several months might have been different. Had I made my life and the lives of my children even more difficult than they needed to be? The question was asked, but could not be answered. I quickly closed my mind to the possibility and tore open my bag of peanuts.

An hour later, the plane touched down in Salt Lake. Fortunately, it wasn't snowing. I picked up a car, dropped Alex off at my brother Dave's house in Holladay, and made the drive to Provo. I'd lived in California long enough now that icy roads made me nervous. No ice today. That was one good thing.

Forty five minutes later, I found myself standing outside the door of my daughter's apartment. I stood there in the chill for a moment, gathering my courage to knock. A few minutes later, I raised my hand tentatively and tapped on the door. One of Alicia's roommates let me in.

I saw my very pregnant, very young, and very vulnerable daughter sitting across the room on the couch, cross stitching a white panel of fabric with the pink letters, "Welcome Jenna." I was moved by Alicia's simple preparation for the arrival of her new daughter. Alicia rose with difficulty, came across the room and put her arms around me. "Thanks for coming, Mom," she said. And we both cried.

Through her tears, I could sense Alicia's happiness over tomorrow's arrival of her little Jenna. In fact, the whole apartment of girls seemed fairly bursting with excitement over the impending birth of my new granddaughter. I recalled last week's words of one of my co-workers: "It doesn't have to matter so much how these little guys get here, Susan. They're still gifts from God." I smiled and hugged her. While I didn't really believe in God anymore, I could certainly appreciate what she was trying to tell me. And she was right: How Jenna got here had now ceased to be of any importance to me.

That night, I lay next to my very uncomfortable Alicia and held her spoon style in my arms. I was so glad I had come. I could smell her favorite fruity shampoo in her hair. And I could feel the baby kicking impatiently under my hand. We were mother and daughter, together again, bonded in a once-in-a-lifetime moment. Neither one of us slept much.

We got up early the next morning. The doctor was going to induce Alicia in a few hours. After dressing, we headed out the door, Alicia's packed suitcase in hand. Almost in spite of myself, I offered a silent prayer for the health and safety of both mother and baby. Ten minutes later, we pulled up in front of Utah Valley Hospital. I let Alicia out at the emergency entrance and went to park the car.

I walked across the cold parking lot and met Alicia at the check in desk. We checked her in and made our way together down the hospital corridor and into the delivery room. The room was decorated to look as homey as possible. In the middle of the room stood a freshly made bed covered with warm, fluffy, white blankets that had just come out of the dryer. It somehow made me feel better that the blankets were warm. Alicia went to the bathroom to undress and put on the hospital gown. When she came out, I tied it for her in the back, after which she climbed into bed to wait for the doctor.

Her best friend Angie joined us a few minutes later. Angie had been very supportive of Alicia, pretty much all of Alicia's life. They grew up together in our neighborhood in Cottonwood Heights. A lot had certainly happened to all of us since then. Angie's parents had divorced as well, although they both remained active in the Church.

I couldn't help but smile as I remembered the day 3-year old Alicia cut 3-year old Angie's hair for her. The unhappy result was short and jagged bangs framing Angie's face, over her otherwise long, straight hair. Alicia came in the house, brandishing her dull, green, Incredible Hulk scissors and was quite proud of herself. Angie didn't seem to mind much, as they both bounced through the door to show me the results. Of course, Angie hadn't yet looked in a mirror.

And now they were both 18 and still fast friends, especially since Alicia's return to Utah. We had left the old neighborhood for California when Alicia was just 9. She was never happy with the move, and she never particularly liked California. She always said that it never felt as though it were home to her. After the divorce, she was especially anxious to go back to what she saw as a better time and place.

Angie walked up to me, gave me a quick hug and hello, and then moved to Alicia's bedside to ask her how she was feeling. By that time her contractions had started, and she was in pain. We called for the doctor, who came in and administered an epidural. The epidural had the unintended effect of putting my daughter completely to sleep. Angie and I sat on either side of Alicia's bed, just watching her sleep through her labor pains. Since both my children are adopted, I'd never been in labor. But I was pretty sure this wasn't how it usually went.

A few hours later, Jenna's head began to crown, and the nurse ran to find the doctor—but not nearly fast enough for me. I tried to wake Alicia. A few minutes later, the doctor entered the room, pulled up the three-legged stool, and wheeled himself under the baby. He shook Alicia awake again and commanded her to, "PUSH. HARD. NOW!"

Seconds later, I was absolutely amazed to see our beautiful and perfect little baby Jenna slip slide her way into the world. I stood there stunned to think that I had just witnessed the birth of a baby—but not just any baby. This baby was my first grandchild. And she really was a miracle.

The doctor quickly snipped the cord and handed our crying Jenna over to the attending nurse. The nurse cleaned her up, weighed her, and efficiently wrapped her in a snug little bundle. Angie and I were so taken with the baby that we failed to see that Alicia had almost slipped off the bed. "Hello," she said. "Hello! Can I get a little help here, please," she pleaded. We soon had Alicia righted in the bed in time for the nurse to place baby Jenna gently into Alicia's arms. We both fell immediately in love with this new little baby girl. She was ours, and we were hers.

When Alicia tired, I took Jenna in my arms and walked our new baby carefully down the corridor to the nursery, not ever wanting to part from her. When we got there, I reluctantly handed Jenna over to the nurse on duty, who placed her in one of those Plexiglas cribs. Jenna was surrounded by dozens of other crying babies. And even though she had a little band on her wrist that said "Swann," I still watched vigilantly to make certain that our name was also affixed to the right little bed.

And then I just stood there, staring at that tiny little bundle of fluff through the window. Someone came up next to me and asked, "Is she your granddaughter?"

"Yes, she's my granddaughter," I replied proudly. "Her name is Jenna." And then involuntarily I thought, Jenna is a child of God, and she is a precious gift to our family. I was overwhelmed for a moment by the wonder of it all.

A few hours later, I kissed my daughter good night, tapped softly on the window at my slumbering granddaughter, and went back to Alicia's apartment to spend the night. It was strange to be at the apartment without Alicia and Jenna. I missed them both already.

What a day it's been, I thought, as I curled up tiredly under the heavy comforter. Jenna had made it into the world with all her fingers and toes. Alicia was safe. "That's all that really matters tonight," I said aloud to no one. So, go to sleep, I said to myself.

But I continued to lay awake thinking about what a tough road Alicia and baby Jenna had ahead of them. I'd been a single mom for almost 2 years now, so I knew a little bit about what it was like to be broke and working to support a child. But I had an education, a good job, and occasional child support payments. Alicia didn't even have a trade. If the odds of success were against me, they were really against her.

And yet I knew how determined Alicia was to do whatever it took to care for her new daughter. She'd written me a letter in January, letting me know she'd made the decision to keep her as yet unborn baby, rather than place her up for adoption. In her letter, she wrote: "There is nothing that says I can't change the odds, if I work hard enough. There is nothing I want more than to give my baby what she deserves." I knew she meant it.

In that same letter, she continued, "I don't think it would hurt anyone, if I had the support of my family." That comment had hit me painfully, as well it should have. Of course she was right. The debate was over. It was her decision to make, and she had made her decision. What she needed now was my full and unequivocal support. I would do whatever I could for her. Now, besides Alicia and Alex, there was baby Jenna to think of. I was emotionally drained. I eventually drifted off into a short and fitful sleep.

The next morning I got up early to go check Alicia and Jenna out of the hospital. It's already Friday, I thought as I got into the car and warmed up the engine. Alex and I had to fly back home Sunday. I'd been off work for almost 3 days now, and I'd taken Alex out of school. We had to go back to California. I hated leaving my daughter in Utah just a few days after she'd had a new baby. But Alicia wanted to stay here.

If I were still someone who counted my blessings, I would have clearly recognized how blessed we were to have the support of my brother Dave and his wife Jaci. They had invited Alicia to come and stay with their family in Holladay for a week, so they could help her recover. So after I picked up Alicia and Jenna from the hospital, we went straight to their home, where Alex was anxiously watching out the window for us to come.

When we arrived at Dave's, everyone was waiting. My nieces and nephews were especially excited to have a new baby in the house. They all took turns holding Jenna, who was snuggled into her slightly over-sized warm, fuzzy, pink onesie, with a little Minnie Mouse logo stitched on the front, oblivious to all the fuss.

My friend Susan came over and brought Jenna a gift and me a hug. Susan had been a close friend when I was married and still living in Salt Lake. Happier times, I thought, as she came through the door, arms open. While distance now separated us, I knew Susan was never very far away, if I needed her. So I was not at all surprised to see her. I was feeling more than a little overwhelmed at the moment and full of mixed feelings, which I didn't need to express to Susan. She just looked at me and knew.

Dave and Jaci also had presents for the new baby. And so did my mom. We spent a happy day together with the new addition to our family. Before Jenna went to bed that night, Jaci got out a big towel and laid it on the kitchen table, so Alicia could give her new baby a sponge bath. Jaci brought out cotton balls, a pan of warm water, baby powder and baby oil. She showed Alicia how to wash her baby carefully, so the cord wouldn't get wet.

When Alex and I left Sunday, it was Jaci who got up and helped Alicia with her 2:00 a.m. feedings. It was Jaci who held Jenna when Alicia needed a nap. It was Jaci who taught Alicia how to be a new mother. It was not me—although I so wanted it to be. This made me very sad, when I thought about it.

When Jaci cooed "Hey, bud," gently to baby Jenna, because her last two babies had been boys, Alicia cooed, "Hey bud," to baby Jenna too. Alicia watched and learned from Jaci. She couldn't have had a better teacher.

A tiring week later, Dave and Jaci took my girls home to Provo. I came as often as I could to see Alicia and Jenna. But for the next 5 years, it was mostly Dave and Jaci who parented Alicia and grand-parented Jenna.

# VII

# Christmas in Sun Valley

*C*hristmas of 1999 was just around the corner. My mom had invited all of us to come to nearby Sun Valley for Christmas. There was nothing she liked better than gathering her family around her. And there was nothing we liked better than being thrown in the same space for several days. Family vacations and get togethers were traditions my parents established when my brothers and I were very young. We were accustomed to traveling and enjoying time together every year.

Growing up, we were fortunate that the Union Pacific Railroad had been one of my dad's clients. What that meant to us were free passes every summer to ride the rails. We traveled as a family to places such as New Orleans, New York, the great Smokey Mountains of Tennessee, Atlanta, and Disneyland.

Since only freight trains ran through our small town of Burley, Idaho, we had to get up at 4:00 a.m. to drive the 24 miles over country roads in the dark to the even smaller town of Minidoka, to catch the passenger trains. Because we were Nielsons, we had to dress up to ride the trains. But we didn't care. We were just happy to be on our way to somewhere—anywhere would do.

My brothers always got new trip hats for our train travel. In the summer, my grandfather Hatch closely buzzed my little brother's heads with his shaver. It was supposedly cooler for them, and it definitely required fewer haircuts. They looked pretty cute all dressed up in their hats, their negligible hair leaving their ears sticking out prominently under their hats. They waved their hats on and off their heads, as my dad rolled the small movie camera.

On the days we left on our train trips, my mom came in to our bedrooms early to wake us up. We rolled sleepily and not yet cheerfully, out of bed. We quickly pulled on our clothes, and my brothers donned their new hats. My dad tossed our bags into the truck of my grandpa's car, and the rest of us went flying out of the house. If the trains were on time, they'd wait for no one.

We were sometimes the only passengers waiting at the little green and white railway station. The train stopped here only if there were passengers to pick up. When the whistle blew, we ran outside and watched the long, yellow train with the red letters on the side chuff and puff its way up to the station, brakes squealing and steam rising from the undercarriage. It was important to avoid the steam. It was very hot, and my dad warned us that it would not hesitate to burn young legs, if we got too close.

When the train came to a full stop, the conductor put out the step for us to climb onto the train. "All Aboard!" He called, checking his pocket watch. "All Aboard!" That was us. We said a quick goodbye to my grandpa and mounted the big steps onto the waiting train. We lugged our bags through several cars, being careful as we crossed the breezeway between the coupled cars, on our way to the Pullman sleepers. After dropping our bags, we were off to the dining car for breakfast.

Later, just before it came time to turn in for the night, the porter pulled our beds out of the wall and turned our couches into sleeping spaces. My brothers and I always wanted to sleep in the upper berths, which was perfectly fine with our parents. Although my dad invariably protested that he wanted to sleep in the upper berths, we knew that he really didn't.

Even when we were back home, and my dad came in from the office for lunch and a short nap as he did every weekday, my two younger brothers bolted into the living room, just as he laid down on his side. One of them called the upper berth and promptly climbed up onto my dad's back. The other one said he'd take the lower berth and curled up next to my dad underneath his arm. Then they all took a short nap together—or at least they pretended to.

We were a train-inspired family both on and off the rails, and we grew up loving traveling of any kind. So when Mom issued the invitation to spend Christmas in Sun Valley, we responded with an enthusiastic, "When do we go?" Mom rented two small condos for our 8 teenagers and one large cabin for the 8 adults and 6 younger boys. There would be 22 of us in all who could make the trip.

Alex and I came in early from California. Alex wanted to spend some time with his cousins at his Uncle Brent and Aunt Marcia's house, so I stayed with Mom. Brent's home had become our extended family home after my dad died and my mom sold her house in Burley and moved to Twin Falls.

Brent's home sat on an acre of mostly grass, with a large garden off to the side. Swing sets, sand boxes, basketball hoops, bikes, small motorized cars, and a riding lawn mower populated the yard. There were a couple of scraggly cats wandering around the place to complete the picture, with a ski boat in the garage. It was a kid's paradise. Alex and I were happy to be in Twin Falls again, in anticipation of our trek to Sun Valley for Christmas. The only thing that would have made it better is if Alicia and Jenna had been able to come, I thought as I drifted off to sleep that night. Just one more day until Christmas.

Christmas Eve morning arrived clear and cold. We all collected early. The cars were lined up out front in the circular driveway, waiting for our four families to caravan to Sun Valley. After a hot breakfast of sticky cinnamon rolls and hot chocolate, we were finally ready to go. We all made a break for the cars after someone shouted, "Bet we'll get there before you do."

As my mom and I climbed into Brent's big Suburban, I suspected that my mom, who was sitting next to me in her new furry brown winter hat, was the happiest of all. Almost all of her family was here. We were missing Alicia, Jenna, and little Brent, who was on a mission in Brazil.

The Nielson clan soon reached the city of Ketchum in the Wood River Valley. I'd been to that little town many times growing up. It had changed some, but not too much. Ketchum was still generally a quaint, former mining town. We decided to stop at Smoky Mountain Pizza for lunch. As we piled inside, we filled up much of the place. It wasn't long before we were stuffing ourselves with warm, family style pizza, crusty, buttery bread, and crisp, chilled salad. The food tasted even better in the cold mountain air.

After we finished lunch, we drove on to Sun Valley, dropping the teens off at their condos. After we unpacked and settled in, some of the adults and most of the kids went sledding. It was a near perfect day for it: the snow was packed solid with a powdery layer of white on top—no ice.

The rest of us went hot tubbing. While it was nice and toasty when we finally reached the water, the tip toe trip from the lockers past the mounded snow banks and out to the hot tub could certainly be described as brisk. We chattered, chatted, and just soaked. Even Mom braved the elements to join us.

After we left the hot tub, we met the others at the ice rink. We watched the professional skaters put on a graceful display of athletic skill. We clapped as they jumped, twirled, and cut criss-crosses in the ice. The kids especially loved watching the Zamboni groom the ice midway through the performance.

As the skaters finished their routines, we could see a torch light ski procession making its way down the face of Mount Baldy. The sun was almost completely down with just small traces of red streaking a back drop against the growing night sky. If the evening had ended there, it would have been a perfect Christmas Eve. But there was still more to come.

We all watched excitedly as a large open sleigh stopped in front of us. "Whoa!" the driver cried, as the horses pawed and stamped their hooves in front of us to stay warm. This is pretty much a Currier and Ives Christmas, I thought to myself, as we all piled in and snuggled together under warm blankets. As we made our way through the snow, it wasn't long before the singing started. Our voices blended together as we rode through the snow, sleigh bells jangling and bright stars twinkling over-head. Predictably, our little 7 and 8 year olds put their own spin on the song "Rudolph"—not the Reindeer, but the bow-legged cowboy. We laughed and sang along with them.

It felt really good to just sing out at the night sky with gusto. I real-ized that I hadn't done much singing in quite some time. But tonight, my spirits soared as I added my voice to the voices of my family. I was also happy that we were on our way to dinner at the Trail Creek Cabin lodge. It was a place Ernest Hemmingway had made famous in the 1930s. I liked Hemmingway's books, and I appreciated his connection to the place we were eating tonight.

I don't remember what we ate for dinner. It was most likely thick, juicy, steaks and loaded baked potatoes: something hearty to ward off the cold. I do remember that there was a roving accordion player, who regaled us with a variety of polkas, folk music, and songs such as, "Lady of Spain." I watched mesmerized as the bellows of his instrument wheezed and his fingers moved proficiently across the many buttons and keys.

When I was little, I wanted to be an accordion player. My parents smiled kindly and encouraged me to stay with the piano. It was certainly the more practical choice. And while I have a piano in my home today that I enjoy playing, there is still something wonderful about the accordion. Maybe it's because accordionists always smile broadly as they play. Maybe it's because they seem to be having such a good time. At any rate, we laughed and sang along with the accordion player. I think I probably sang the loudest.

When we finally got back to our cabin later that night, we opened the traditional Christmas pajamas, or in Alex's case, what passed as pajamas but were really "Yo Quiero Taco Bell" boxer shorts. He pulled them on over his pants and posed for pictures with his cousins.

In the spirit of a true Idaho Christmas, Marcia had bought each of us a wooden, painted ornament that was made locally. We all hung them on the Christmas tree, filling its green branches. Alex got a friendly, goofy looking Rudolph, with the obligatory big red nose. My ornament was a deep, purplish color cut in the shape of the state of Idaho. I loved it.

Then one of my brothers read from Luke, as my dad always had each Christmas Eve. "And it came to pass in those days that there went out a decree from Caesar Augustus that all the world should be taxed." Believer or not, I still found comfort in the words, "And suddenly there was with the angels a multitude of heavenly host praising God, and saying, Glory to God in the highest, and on earth, peace, good will toward men." I listened to those familiar words as the fire popped and cracked in the fire place, throwing light on the upturned faces of my nieces and nephews, who listened appreciatively to the words of Luke. On some level, I almost regretted not having that child-like faith.

The little guys eventually tired, and before we packed them off to bed, we knelt together in family prayer. I resisted inwardly, but I participated nonetheless. It's too bad I don't believe as they do anymore, I thought. I missed that spiritual connection with my family.

As things quieted down, I walked out on the upstairs balcony for a breath of quiet night air. It had been a really wonderful Christmas Eve, I marveled to myself. And I wished that my dad could have been here to enjoy his beautiful grandchildren. He would have loved them so much. My dad always used those same words to tell us about his own father, who had also died at the age of 60. None of his grandchildren ever knew him either.

It was then that the words to my dad's favorite Christmas song flooded my mind, as they do every year about this time: "I'll be home for Christmas." At least one of us is home in Idaho with the family, Dad, I thought.

And then I wondered what my dad would think about the course my life had taken. I knew he would still love me, because he always had. I knew he would still refer to me fondly as "Princess," just as he always did. But would he still be proud of me? I wasn't sure. Not really wanting to know the answer, I tucked that particular question away for another time. It was Christmas Eve. It was a time to be happy. I knew my dad would agree with me on that score.

"I love you, Dad," I said softly through tears, looking up at the night sky. "Merry Christmas." Then I turned to go back inside.

# VIII

## The Gurgling Cod

*A*nother bright light in my life at the time was my long-time friend and home teacher, Mark Boud. Even before the divorce, Mark and I had worked together in the Young Women's/ Young Men's program, when I was still active in the Church. I was also friends with his wife Kate. Even more importantly, Alex knew and loved Mark, Kate, and their children. And they loved him. Their children were younger than Alex and they thought he was "cool." Alex was a kind, good-looking boy, who didn't know he was a kind, good-looking boy. Ever since he was a baby, I had thought of him as my gentle giant. Most everyone loved Alex. The Bouds were no exception.

When Alex and I walked into the Boud's home for Sunday dinner, which we did on a regular basis, we could count on smelling something tasty cooking on the stove or baking in the oven. Sometimes there were even warm rolls with butter to go along with the main course and salad. The big table in the dining room was set with white linens, as if the Bouds were expecting special guests. As we came through the door, the kids within ear shot of the door bell ran out to say hello and welcome us inside.

The Boud home was comfortable. The kind of place where I could feel free to take off my shoes and just sink into a chair. No questions asked. For me, their home was a little island of peace. A port in the storm, as it were, where I could spend a few hours letting someone else take care of things, just for a little while.

When I moved out of the house after the divorce, I wanted to keep Alex as close as possible to the old neighborhood where his friends lived. So I chose an apartment complex that wasn't too far away. As a consequence, we were still in the same ward boundaries. Not that I went to church much. But Bishop Reese asked Mark to continue to be our home teacher. I don't think Mark would have had it any other way. I don't think I would have either.

Mark didn't just visit us. He became part of our lives and incorporated us into his family. It would be difficult to find anyone more generous than Mark and Kate Boud. So having Sunday dinner with the Boud family was a pretty regular event for me and Alex.

I enjoyed helping Kate complete the last minute meal preparations in the kitchen, or just sitting on the bar stool next to the counter and talking with her, while she applied the finishing touches to dessert. Sometimes her mom Shirley would be there visiting from Canada. I loved Shirley. She was well read and quick witted, with a ready sense of humor that she shared liberally. Kate was similar to her mom in those respects. Kate, Shirley, and I had lots of good laughs together. I found that when I was with them, I could still find things to laugh about.

One of the most captivating things about our Sunday dinners at the Bouds was a rather unique water pitcher that Kate bought on a trip to Boston. The pitcher was blue and painted to look similar to a cod—buggy eyes, scales and all. When the cod was filled with water, tipped just right to pour the water into waiting glasses, and then tipped back up again, the cod gurgled loudly. I'm not sure what principles of physics made the cod gurgle. And when it came right down to it, I really didn't want to know. Explaining it might take the mystery out of it.

Alex and the other children would wait with anticipation during our Sunday dinners, as the gurgling cod made its way to the dinner table. When the water was poured and the cod gurgled, it never failed to elicit laughter from everyone. And there was no shortage of young volunteers to fill the empty water glasses, as long as they could use the gurgling cod.

After steaming bowls of plentiful food were placed on the table, we eagerly took our seats. Mark asked us to all join hands as we sat around the table. He talked about how happy they were to have Alex and me join them for dinner. Once our hands were securely clasped together, Mark would ask someone to offer a blessing on the food. Often one of his children. Sometimes Mark or Kate. Whoever said the blessing invariably expressed gratitude for their friendship with Alex and me.

As the blessing ended, there was lots of happy eating, good conversation, and more laughter. I appreciated those shared meals in the home of good friends. So did Alex. It all felt pretty normal and nice to be part of a family again that went beyond the two of us, just for a little while. The Boud family patiently loved and accepted us, year in and year out. Always they waited for something that would touch our hearts and bring us back to the Church. They would have to wait for a very long time.

Mark typically didn't "count" our dinners as fulfilling his home teaching obligation. In fact, I never felt as though we were an obligation to Mark. He came. He cared. He listened. He offered a short, spiritual thought. He read a scripture. He asked Alex about school. He wanted to know what he could do to help. He hugged us when he arrived and when he left. He was always there if we needed him.

What Mark didn't do was almost as important to me as what he did do: he never pushed, probed, or prodded. He didn't judge. He just loved us. Mark was the charity in my life that "never faileth."

It wasn't just Sunday dinners that found me in the Boud home. Mark and Kate enjoyed entertaining friends. I was invited to more than one of the mostly couples parties they gave. They didn't think to leave me out just because I was now single and inactive. For me, the highlight of the parties at the Bouds was not the food, the ambiance, or the good company. It was the competitive word games.

One of Kate's favorite games involved cutting up strips of paper, asking someone to write the names of famous politicians, historical figures, or entertainers on the papers, folding the papers in half, and placing the folded names in a large bowl. After the party goers divided into teams, one designated team member would select a name from the bowl. Without saying or spelling the name, or giving an overt clue, the team member on tap had to find ways to describe the person to his team. Playing the game was fun. Watching it being played was even more fun.

Almost inevitably, the people with Kate on their team won. Kate's very competitive when she plays games. She takes no prisoners. I like that about her. The only person who has a chance of beating her is Shirley. So, to level the play field, Mark tried to make sure those two were never on the same team.

Mark helped Alex and me in other ways as well. He's a real estate economist, so not surprisingly, he's very savvy about the value of property. Five years after Alex and I moved into an apartment, and two years after my bankruptcy was discharged, my mom loaned me money for a down payment on a house. I went looking for something to buy.

I found a two bedroom, two bath townhome in nearby Aliso Viejo with a two-car tandem garage. It was still under construction. It had an office area, a fireplace, and an island in the kitchen. There was one unit left in the current phase that I could afford. Next week, the prices went up. So I put down earnest money—and called Mark.

He assured me that I was on the right track. "Go for it, Susan," he said. "It's a great buy in a good area. I don't think you can go wrong." It was helpful to get my decision confirmed from someone who knew what he was talking about. I still wasn't quite used to making decisions this big by myself. As it turned out, Mark was right.

I was elated to think that we might be able to have our own place again. And it was new! My offer was eventually accepted, and with my credit back in good shape, and my job stable, I qualified for a low down, FHA-insured loan. At first Alex wasn't sure he wanted to leave Laguna Niguel. But Aliso was right next door. And by now he had his own small truck, so he was pretty independent. Alex soon grew to love the place as much as I did. The garage in particular became Alex's domain—now called "the man cave." The place was ours. And it was home.

I went by the construction site at least a couple of times a week to observe the progress and take pictures of our new home as it went up. As I walked around the site, I grew to love the smell of cut wood. To this day, the scent of sawdust makes me happy.

I was excited when the house was finally framed. I was thrilled when the drywall was finished and delighted when the fireplace insert was set in place. Day by day, I walked up and down the stairs after the workmen left and ran my hand along the dust in the new oak railings. One of my friends commented that my new place seemed small to her. I thought it was a palace.

Several months passed. By December of 2000, we were ready to move in. Of course we couldn't afford movers or a truck rental. I didn't even have to call Mark to ask him for help. He had already arranged it. Mark and his son Brenden, men from the Church with trucks, Alex with his new/old truck, and my brother Norm had us all moved in several hours later. It helped that we didn't really have that much to move, I suppose. As I lay in bed that night, I could hardly go to sleep. I was deliciously tired. What a Christmas this would be, I marveled. What a phenomenal way to begin the New Year.

The only sad part of our move was that we weren't in Mark's ward anymore. So he couldn't be our home teacher. But he didn't let that stop him. Mark kept in touch. He invited me to go with him and Kate to wedding receptions where we were both invited. He made sure I was included.

Eventually he and Kate moved their family to a new development in San Clemente. It was a beautiful home with a lovely back yard. Now we get invited to dinner in their new home. And of course for us, dinner still isn't dinner in the Boud home without the gurgling cod.

# IX

## Sunrise on Haleakala

*A*lex and I were just getting comfortably settled into our new townhome and starting to plan for his high school graduation in June, when my boss asked me if I'd be willing to take a short-term assignment in Hawaii working with the Department of Education. "You're asking me to go to Hawaii and work?" I asked her in absolute disbelief.

"That's right," she replied rather nonchalantly, I thought, as if she'd just asked me to take a drive to downtown Burbank. "We'd need you to be in Honolulu for about 9 months. Obviously we'd pay all of your expenses, and we'll fly you home, say about every 3 weeks. What do you say?"

I could scarcely believe that I was actually being offered a work assignment in Hawaii. Alex was leaving for college in September, so he wouldn't be home. And I was dreading having him gone. Now I could be gone too! And who turns down an assignment to work in Hawaii? So of course I said, "Yes!"

I spent the first few months in a hotel before I found a reasonably priced, one-bedroom place at the Ilikai Marina on the west end of Waikiki Beach. The interior was nice enough, although fairly unremarkable. But when I pulled opened the drapes to the balcony, I had a full view of the ocean, with Diamond Head off to the left and Waikiki Beach almost straight in front of me. It was stunning. I rented it the first day I saw it.

A few weeks later, after helping Alex take his stuff to the dorms at San Diego State for the fall semester, and bidding him an embarrassing and tearful "mom good-bye," I packed in earnest for the move to the Ilikai. I was all set to fly out of Los Angeles the morning of September 11, 2001.

I turned on the television to catch the early-morning news. As I finished loading my suitcase, I saw what everyone else who was watching the news at that early hour saw: The second plane fly into the twin trade towers in New York City. There's no way to describe either what I witnessed or felt. And there's no need to. Everyone who lives in the United States vividly remembers that day and all its horrors. It was so surreal. And yet very real to those people who lost their lives, and to others who lost precious loved ones.

Similar to anyone else who planned to fly anywhere that day, my flight to Honolulu was canceled. My company booked me out on a flight 3 days later. I had to get back to work. Hawaii was now where I worked, and it was where I needed to be. Like everyone else, I was scared to death at the thought of getting on a plane. It didn't matter much that I was going to the lovely island of Oahu, I hated leaving home, friends, and family behind.

When I got to LAX, I'd never seen the airport so quiet, or so empty. There still weren't that many planes flying. And most of them were not flying full. I was booked on American Airlines. When I got on board, I called my mom before takeoff. I just needed to hear her voice. The mood on board was somber. Crew members had just lost friends. No one spoke unless it was absolutely necessary. We were all still in a state of shock, and we weren't certain if some other terrible thing might be just about to happen.

When I finally landed safely in Honolulu and picked up a car for the drive to the Ilikai, I had a much different feeling when I got to my apartment and looked out at the wide, blue ocean. It was still beautiful, but it now also represented the vast amount of distance between me and everything I loved. If something happened, it might be impossible to get home.

But I was here now. And life had to go on, just as it did everywhere else. Work kept me busy during the day. On Saturdays I tried to get out and see Honolulu, or just drive around the island of Oahu, which only took a few hours. My time here was limited, and I wanted to see as much of the island as possible.

Every morning when I woke up, and every evening before dinner, I dragged my white plastic chair out onto the balcony and just sat and looked at the ocean. Sometimes I saw little sparkles of light glinting off the water. At other times, there were white sail boats traversing the blue expanse in front of me. The brilliant orange and red sunsets were nothing short of spectacular. There's no doubt that I was living in paradise. I was only sorry that I had no one here to share it with. So I said things to myself like, "That sunset is amazing!"

On Sunday mornings, since I was no longer religious or going to church, I got into the habit of walking several blocks to the local Denny's restaurant over on Kuhi Avenue for breakfast. The routine was somehow comforting.

On one particular Sunday morning, I walked home from breakfast along the beach past the Hilton Hawaiian Village. Adjacent to the Hilton Hawaiian Village, out on the beach, I saw a knot of people dressed in Aloha shirts and shorts, some in muumuus and flip flops, most of them singing. I drew closer to see what was happening.

It seemed that they were all worshipping God on the beach, amid microphones and sound systems. It was literally an ocean side "come as you are" service. Curious, I pulled up a large rock and sat down, removed my Rainbow sandals, and pushed my toes into the warm, white sand.

A woman in a tapered blue and white flowered Hawaiian dress was performing a beautiful gospel hula to taped music. I watched the lovely movements of her expressive hands, with the swaying green palms as back drop. I could feel the warm trade winds gently caress my back. It was a lovely morning. There were a few more Christian songs sung live by gentle and mellifluous male voices. Some of the men played guitars or ukuleles, while seemingly unphased sunbathers sat just beyond them, closer to the water.

Looking around, I saw a sign that read: Waikiki Beach Chaplaincy: Church on the Beach. I found out later that this church met right here on the beach every Sunday, as they'd apparently done every year since 1970. Their web site said that their services were "intended for those who would never venture into the doorway of a church." That pretty much fit me at this point in my life. So instead of going to church, church came to me. Worked for me, although I'm not sure why, since I was no longer a believer.

One Sunday, one of the volunteers was passing out copies of what they called, "The Living New Testament." So I took a copy. I still have it. It's a contemporary version of the New Testament. The front cover of the book has a picture of the ocean in the foreground with Diamond Head and Waikiki in the background. The back cover continues with pictures of sailboats and the Waikiki hotels, including the familiar rainbow markings of the Hilton Hawaiian Village. The words on the front and spine of the book read, "The Greatest is Aloha." And "Aloha is love."

In addition to the weekly songs and dances, there was always a short sermon. It usually focused on things such as grace and mercy, or perhaps referenced "acts of Aloha." Almost any kind and generous act, including a hug, can be considered an act of Aloha. In the Hawaiian language, the word "aloha" means things such as love, mercy, and compassion. It was only later that the word came to be used as a greeting.

The services were non-denominational Christian. Their ministry policy was to "give the opportunity for non-believers to find faith." I didn't really expect to find my missing faith here, or anywhere else for that matter. But for whatever reason, I still liked coming to their services, which I continued to do just about every Sunday that I was in Honolulu for the next 6 months.

I couldn't explain my actions even to myself, so I didn't try. I just knew that it made me feel good to come here, so I did. It was a simple weekly touch with someone else's sacred that happened on one of the world's most beautiful islands.

I had one other particular touch in Hawaii with something I found sacred, a few years later, when I was no longer living on the island of Oahu. This one happened on the island of Maui. I had gone there to spend a week at the Marriott Maui Ocean Club on Ka'anapali Beach. It was a beautiful place with white sands and turquoise waters, with an amazing swimming pool that seemingly went on forever as it snaked in and around palm trees and man-made black rocks.

But there was something else I wanted to do. I wanted to see the sun rise over the massive volcanic mountains of Haleakala. Haleakala means "House of the Sun." I had read that anciently, this mountain was the province only of high priests. It was a sacred place where they went to receive spiritual wisdom. For my part, I just wanted to see the sun come up.

I looked for and found a tour that would take me there. It required getting up at 3:00 a.m. and taking a 2-hour bus ride in the dark up a curving mountain road. I brought along a jacket and a blanket, because the clerk at the front desk told me the outside temperature on the mountain at that time of the day would be 40 degrees at best.

We arrived on the mountain about 30 minutes before sunrise. There were maybe 75 or 100 of us standing out there on the edge of the mountain, waiting for the sun to come up. It was very dark, cold, and cloudy. I had heard that a cloudy morning might mean more color in the sky. I expectantly wrapped my blanket around me, tucked my hands into its folds, and tried to keep warm. The weather up here was such a contrast to the warm, balmy temperatures in Ka'anapali down below.

As the dawn approached, a park ranger read the words to the mele oli, chanted anciently by an old Kahuna. Standing out there in the dark with the coming of the light, it felt kind of magical. Translated, the mele oli says: Awaken/Arise. The sun in the east, from the ocean, the ocean deep. Climbing to the heaven, the heaven highest in the east. There is the sun. Awaken!

As if on cue, the peach, orange, red, and mauve rays of the sun began breaking through the clouds. The colors set against the black rock of the volcano and the white clouds below were breath-taking. With the exception of cameras clicking, there was complete silence on the mountain. We were in awe at the majesty unfolding before us. I have never seen a sunrise such as that before or since. I thought that if there were a God, and I could feel his presence, it would be here on the mountains of Haleakala.

# X

# Light of the World

*I* was sitting in the airport in Honolulu one day, waiting for a flight home to California. My attention was drawn to the TV monitor, where the broadcast feed was coming from Salt Lake City. The announcer was describing the city's preparations for the upcoming 2002 Winter Olympic Games. The pictures and commentary made the Olympic events look and sound both festive and exciting.

I'd never been to an Olympics—summer or winter. And now here they were, practically in my own backyard. Why not go? I asked myself. You can afford the flight, I continued my interior monologue. I'm sure Dave and Jaci would let you stay with them. There was no one else I needed to consult with at this point in my life. "Why not go!" I said emphatically, this time likely out loud, judging by the faces of the waiting passengers sitting nearest me.

The day I flew into Salt Lake City for the Olympics, I barely recognized the place, even though I'd once lived there for years. There were flags flying everywhere, colorful displays, and burning torches. There was a collective energy, a sense of anticipation, and an exuberant light-heartedness that I have never experienced in any city before or since.

Everyone was moving around purposefully. Olympic athletes walked the streets, laughing and talking but still seemingly focused on their upcoming events. There were people here literally from all over the world swelling the ranks of the local Utah residents. The diversity was incredible. It was such an exhilarating time and place to be!

I had seen a sign on a passing bus as I came in from the airport. It carried a picture of the conference center on its side, announcing a production called, "The Light of the World." It was being staged by the Church and promised to be a multi-cultural event. That might be a fun thing to do, I thought. So I got a ticket.

As I came through the doors of the conference center that Saturday night in February to watch what had been billed as a huge multi-media production, the halls and portals were filled with performers from countries all over the world. They were twirling flags, dancing, and singing.

I made my way inside and took my seat alone in the packed hall. The place had been completely transformed. Up in front rested a huge stage covered with a sheer, white curtain that partially obscured the back side of the stage. There were large projectors and sound systems everywhere.

As I read my program, it said: "Light of the World: Celebration of Light." And then, "Spirit of Man/Glory of God." At least I believed in the spirit of man. I saw myself now as something of a humanist: the idea being that everyone has some contribution he or she can make to society. God was not part of the equation for me. But I could perhaps appreciate the notion of God, I thought, as the lights dimmed.

The place went completely dark. Suddenly there were asteroids, astral projections of nebulae, and shooting stars that went whizzing around and across the stage. The choral and orchestral overture was punctuated by the booming announcer's voice: "Let there be light." And there was light. A montage of filmed images followed, beginning with multi-colored fish, flowers, and all kinds of animal life. I recognized the creative periods from Genesis. This presentation was to begin, appropriately enough, in the beginning.

Folk dancers from all over the world spilled onto the stage, coming from nations such as Japan, Russia, Africa, and China, as the loud speakers thundered: "The universal spirit of man shines with the glory of God." This is going to be an amazing production, I thought, even for a church that is no stranger to amazing productions. The dancers parted and members of the Mormon Tabernacle Choir streamed onto the stage singing something such as: "Come Ye Nations of the Earth." Whatever their exact words were, the song clearly conveyed the sense of a world-wide church.

I had only been gone 8 years. But apparently there were some things that had changed while I was away. There would be even more changes before I came back to the Church 7 years later. After I came back, my friend Soni asked me if I were surprised that things had changed in my absence. I told her that I was.

"Do you mean to tell me," she said, "that you thought this growing and changing Church was just standing still while you were away?" she asked me incredulously. When she put it that way, it did sound kind of ridiculous. But that was exactly what I thought. I thought that the Church I left would be the same church I came back to. And that I would be the same person I was when I left. I couldn't have been more wrong on either count.

The large, white curtains on the stage in front of me parted, revealing a little baby crying in a cradle. His parents were singing one of the many original songs written for this production: "Do You Know Who You Are?" The age-old question, I thought, as pictures of beautiful little children from the world over played across the wide movie screen.

And then the voice of a little girl coming from out of the darkness— I'm glad they chose to begin with a girl, I thought—Her voice spoke about being lost in a fog and groping her way toward shore. I could relate metaphorically to that idea. Her words ended with something about the light of love that "shone on her in that very hour." It was Helen Keller.

More light, color, and sound as costumed children flew, twisted, and tumbled in the air above the stage, the ropes barely visible from where I sat. The children then chanced upon a large "Book of Life." As they opened its pages, their own "journey of discovery" began.

The audience was introduced to a character by the name of Alma Richards—a nice, solid, Mormon name, I reflected. I wonder if he's real. Alma was running away from his home in Parowan, Utah. That sounded real enough. He met up with a man called Dr. True Blood, who was also waiting for passage on a ship. It turned out that these men were both historical figures, and their meeting a matter of record. Dr. True Blood encouraged Alma to go home and get an education. He told him that no one ever found his destiny by running away. Words to live by, I thought.

Then Alma sang: "Where Is My Path?" His voice, similar to all the others in the cast, was both trained and resonantly beautiful. This production rivals something I might see on Broadway, I thought, entranced. Then there was a flashback to Alma's ancestors in England, and the movie screen filled with people boarding a ship to America to join the saints. My ancestors had done the same thing. And I had once been intensely proud of their faith and their strength. I had since come to believe that they must have either been duped or delusional for following a dreamer such as Joseph Smith. Which was it: strong and faithful, or duped and delusional, I wondered?

As pictures of people boarding the ships from England passed over the screen, the voice of Charles Dickens came through the speakers as if in answer to my question. Dickens called this large body of Mormon emigrants "the pick and flower of England." I had both read and taught many of Charles Dickens' books. I had a high regard for him and his work. I had never before heard that statement. I later verified its authenticity. Charles Dickens had indeed referred to the English saints as the "pick and flower of England." That was quite a compliment. I liked that.

As the ships on screen docked, people dressed as early pioneers symbolically moved westward across the stage, pulling their handcarts as the wind and snow whistled around them. The actors on stage were accompanied by film footage depicting the freezing, starvation, and death of the saints at Sweetwater.

One man then sat alone on the stage and sang: "Lead Kindly Light." That was my favorite hymn. I had always loved the words: "The night is dark, and I am far from home. Lead thou me on." I no longer believed in a "thou" that either would or could lead me on. Just so much wishful thinking, I said to myself. But the song was lovely and the man's voice singing the song sounded both hopeful and wistful as he sang the familiar words.

As the Sweetwater rescue ended, a youthful Brigham Young proclaimed that "the house of the Lord will be established in the tops of the mountains, and all nations shall flow unto it." He was certainly right about that, I mused. And then people of all nations, creeds, and colors flowed once again onto the large stage, this time collectively singing, "Come, Come, Ye Saints." I was deeply moved by the still familiar words, "All is well. All is well."

Then I remembered reading that the Church was rebuilding the temple in Nauvoo. I was strangely and inexplicably drawn to the idea of a temple in Nauvoo. I had even thought about trying to go to the open house, which would be taking place in June of this same year. Historical interest, perhaps. Or maybe it was because I appreciated the sense of poetic justice that the Mormons, who had once been driven from Nauvoo, were now reclaiming part of their heritage.

Part of my heritage too. I had ancestors who were married in the Nauvoo temple just before they had been expelled from their city, only to have their sacred and beautiful temple burned to the ground. I had visited Nauvoo with my family when I was in my early teens. I remembered arguing with a member of the Community of Christ church (RLDS) who tried to tell me that no ordinance work had been done in the Nauvoo temple. "Of course it was," I told him. "Some of my relatives were married there." He didn't believe me, and I didn't care. It had still happened just as I said it did.

My attention returned again to the creation on stage, which had now cut to the account of a female athlete named Tenley Albright. I appreciated the equal treatment women received in this production. I had never heard of Tenley Albright, who in 1956, after overcoming an early childhood bout with polio, went on to become the first American woman to win a gold medal in ladies single figure skating in the Olympics. That by itself would have been an incredible accomplishment. But she did not stop there. Tenley Albright also went to Harvard medical school and became a surgeon. Both of her ambitious dreams were realized. By highlighting Tenley's story, the Church, which seemed to be enlarging before my eyes, was sending a message to little girls everywhere: "You can be anything you want to be."

Just when I was wondering how the whole Alma Richards story and his pioneer ancestors were going to tie in to stories of Olympic athletes, we returned to the story of Alma Richards, now an athlete and Olympic gold medal winner in the Stockholm games of 1912. He had gone back to school and become a world-class runner. Film footage showed Alma kneeling in prayer before his event. A courageous gesture, I thought.

And then Dante Alighieri's voice: "This is the spark that then extends into a vivid flame, and, like a star in heaven, glows in me." Followed by the voice of Isaiah: "Arise, shine, for your light is come." Bright lights then swept the audience as performers filled the aisles, carrying lanterns of light. A projection of the Christus statue fell on the white curtain. The Christus that stands across the street at the Temple Square Visitor's Center.

The same Christus I visited often when I was studying at the University of Utah. At that time, I came because it was a place where I could find peace when my own light faded. I had forgotten. I had forgotten. But that was then, and this is now, I reasoned.

The whole stage overflowed with people holding candles aloft, who were soon joined again by the Tabernacle Choir, dressed in white, also carrying candles. They sang, "High on a Mountain Top," as the projection on the screen changed to a picture of the Wasatch Mountains. I loved those mountains. As the choir sang the words, "Her light should there attract the gaze, of all the world in latter days," the flags of all nations held by the peoples of the world moved into the audience, amid sounds of thunderous applause.

We all jumped to our feet, clapping our hands in admiration. What an inspiring and flawless performance! In spite of myself, I was filled with a sense of pride for these people in my church. In many ways, they were still part of me, even though I was no longer part of them. The original songs and music, interspersed with stirring and familiar hymns, had brought me to tears: the spirit of man . . . the glory of God.

I was sorry to leave Salt Lake City behind when I flew out Monday night. It was an experience I would take with me for the rest of my life. As wonderful as it all had been, I thought often of the huge multi-media theatrical production that I'd seen at the conference center that highlighted the achievements of artists, humanitarians, scientists and yes, even the Mormon pioneers.

And I continued to grope my way forward, until, just as Helen Keller, the light of love would "shine on me in that very hour."

# XI

# Kindred Spirits

*M*y friend Marilyn invited me to come with her and one of her other client/friends, whom I didn't know, along with two of her friend's friends, only one of whom Marilyn knew, to have dinner and watch a play in Costa Mesa. The whole thing sounded complicated to me, but the idea, as Marilyn explained it, was for 5 of us who didn't all know each other to come together for an evening and see a comedy titled: *Five Women Wearing the Same Dress.*

The play was about five bridesmaids who were stuck wearing the same ugly and tasteless dress at the society wedding of a bride, whom none of them really liked. The five bridesmaids eventually escaped the reception and found refuge in a bedroom upstairs, where they shared their secrets and their often hilarious outlook on life. The 5 women soon came to realize that even with all their differences, they had more in common with each other than they did with the bride. It sounded similar to an episode of Seinfeld to me. A play "about nothing" in terms of a plot. But as the house lights dimmed, I found the characters colorful, and their interactions fun to watch.

I had to admit it was a pretty creative idea to replicate the plot of the play in some small way by inviting 5 women who didn't all know each other to spend an evening together and find out what they had in common. It was similar to a play within a play. And I love plays of either variety. So I agreed to go along.

Marilyn's other client/friend who joined us that night was named Soni. I found that she was a woman with whom I had a lot in common. Just as I was, Soni was divorced with two children. Just as I had been, Soni had been left with big tax bills that she knew nothing about. And similar to me, Soni had both a background in English and psychology. But unlike me, Soni is Jewish and still a practicing member of her faith.

We clicked almost immediately, somewhere, I think, during intermission. Soni was warm and friendly. She could talk with anyone about anything. Me included. And talk we did, and still do. We have what we call a long "running conversation with lags" that we can pick up again at a moment's notice.

In addition to loving plays, Soni and I both really enjoyed movies. Especially unusual movies with complex characters. The kind that typically didn't play at the more mainstream theaters, but which we could almost always find in some off-the-beaten path theatre in either Irvine or Costa Mesa. More fun than the movies was the dialogue afterward. We spent hours analyzing and picking the movies and characters apart. It was our idea of a good time.

As we got to know each other better, our conversations quite naturally turned to family and, from my perspective at the time, quite unnaturally to religion. Soni is not only a religious person herself; she is a student of world religions. As a student of religions, she knows a lot about the Mormons. She respected my culture, and she often told people of her faith that if they wanted to witness the birth of a major world religion, they should watch the Mormons. She grew curious as to why I had left my faith behind.

Curious and concerned, but never critical. In fact, she understood me very well. She knew that I was on a journey to somewhere, although neither of us knew quite where yet. This bothered me far more than it did her. If there was ever anyone who believed in and respected personal journeys, it was Soni. It would just take time to unfold, she told me.

I reminded Soni over and over that I was no longer a believer. But I wasn't particularly convincing when I couldn't seem to stop being interested in things spiritual. She saw that in me more quickly than I saw it in myself. Soni told me in no uncertain terms that she believed that I was a spiritual person. And that our meeting was "beshert." She told me that was Yiddish for fated, or meant to be.

I no longer thought that anything in life was "meant to be," but I couldn't explain away my connection to Soni. She seemed to have my best interest at heart. Even Alex called her his "wing woman," when she talked me down off the cliff over some of his "growing moments." But spiritual? Me? I didn't think so.

"What?" I asked her incredulously one day. "You think I'm still a spiritual person? I don't even believe in God, let alone my own religion. No one else I know thinks I'm spiritual. You may be wrong about that." My words were tantamount to throwing a flaming gauntlet down at her feet. Neither one of us likes being wrong about anything, even though we know we often are.

"I'm not wrong about this, Susan," she insisted. "I see you as I see Jacob. You're wrestling with an angel. You're questioning and searching. In the Jewish tradition, questioning God is what it means to be spiritual."

That put a whole different spin on what it meant to be spiritual, I thought to myself. I was certainly questioning and searching. That part was true.

Soni continued, "People who have stopped wondering and stopped asking questions. Those people are not spiritual. That's not you. You're a very spiritual person, Susan."

For some very odd reason, it made me feel good to think that someone I knew thought I was spiritual. I actually liked the idea that I might be wrestling with an angel. Even though I didn't believe in angels. I wisely didn't share this particular idea with anyone else.

I knew my thoughts were contradictory. But whose thoughts aren't? Some of the most highly evolved intellectual beings I know can hold two contradictory thoughts in their minds at the same time. I remembered something I once heard the author Alice Walker say at a conference: "Take your contradictions and wrap them around you like a shawl." I loved that idea. Maybe contradictions weren't such a bad thing after all? So I stopped agonizing over my contradictions and continued to wrestle with angels I didn't believe in.

One of Soni's other favorite ways to keep me in touch with the sacred was to invite me to her home for the Passover Seder. She saw all her friends as fellow travelers, regardless of their religious persuasions. So it wasn't unusual for her family and Jewish friends to end up with an assortment of Catholics, Protestants, and even me—the Mormon—at dinner.

I loved taking part in the tradition of the Passover Seder. After we were seated and the candles were lit, we were given copies of the Haggadah. We all participated in reading the story of the ancient Israelite liberation from slavery in Egypt. We began the Seder ritual with the youngest child asking the question: "Why is this night different than all other nights?" A passage from Exodus seemed to best answer that question: "And you shall tell it to your son on that day, saying, 'Because of this God did for us when He took me out of Egypt.'" (Exodus 13:8).

As we read, I sometimes thought about the Mormon exodus from the Midwest. Similar to the Jews, we were also driven out of our lands and into the desert. Unlike the Jews, we hadn't been slaves. But we had been persecuted. I could relate to the Jewish exodus, at least on some level, I thought.

We sang Passover songs. I liked singing the songs, even though I couldn't always pronounce the Hebrew words. The Jewish Midrash says that there are 10 levels of prayer, and then there's music. I think that's true. We had no shortage of singing at Soni's Seder dinners.

When we finished the Seder plate, Soni brought out a mouth-watering salmon dinner, complete with salad, vegetables, and matzo dumplings. I ate and enjoyed the conversation, which usually turned to politics. After we further stuffed ourselves with an array of desserts, the youngest person looked for the afikoman. Sometimes it was Soni's son, Rick. At other times, it was her cousin's grandchild.

I didn't understand it all. But I appreciated it all. As Tevye said in one of my favorite plays, *Fiddler on the Roof,* "Our traditions tell us who we are and what God wants from us." Every year, I enjoyed the ritual and the tradition of the Passover Seder dinner at Soni's home. I always felt welcome and included. And I grew to love Soni's sons, Joe and Rick, just as she loved Alex.

The years passed. Our friendship and conversations about both family and religion continued. Sometimes over dinner. Sometimes not. Soni is a very smart person. And she believes in God. Most really smart people I associated with at the time didn't think a smart person believed in God or anything that was "unseen." They were too sophisticated for that.

I told Soni that I didn't believe in God anymore either. I don't think she ever once believed that to be true.

And then came an event that neither Soni nor I anticipated. It was 2004. The year Mel Gibson released his film, *The Passion of the Christ*.

It didn't surprise me that Soni wanted to see it. Nor did it surprise me that she asked me to go with her. I had read about some of the controversy surrounding the film, mostly about criticisms over anti-Semitism. I knew Soni would want to see for herself and form her own opinion, as she always did. For my part, I had heard that the film was primarily filmed in Italy and that the dialogue was mostly in reconstructed Aramaic with subtitles. My interest in the film was most definitely intellectual. We went to see the movie together.

I sat in the darkened theater waiting for the film to begin, with Soni by my side. I checked my watch to see if it was about time for the movie to start. Not much longer now, I thought. I yawned involuntarily once or twice and hoped I wouldn't have trouble staying awake. I needn't have worried.

The movie opened in the Garden of Gethsemane, with Jesus uttering aloud the words, "Adoni, Adoni." I could feel the pain of his loneliness as he went to find his sleeping disciples. No one was watching with him. He was completely alone—until the wraithlike Satan appeared, weaving himself around Jesus and whispering doubts in his ear. Jesus was now not only without friends, he was in the presence of his arch enemy. I sat up straighter in my seat. My feelings of concern heightened as I watched the scene unfold.

Satan was portrayed as a pale faced, thin man with a smooth, hairless face, cloaked in black. His voice was high and reedy. Satan asked Christ the questions: "Who is your father? Who are you?" He smirked at him with an intense, knowing stare, as a snake slithered from under his cloak toward Jesus.

As the snake got closer, Jesus rose from his prayers and crushed the head of the snake under the heel of his sandal. As I rejoiced over the symbolic demise of the snake, I realized that I was quickly losing my intellectual distance from the unfolding events.

The soldiers came. Jesus was betrayed by a kiss from his friend and disciple, Judas. Peter cut off the ear of one of the guards, and Jesus restored it. Jesus was then lead off in ropes, chains, and shackles to face his accusers. By the next scene, I was enthralled.

John ran to find Jesus' mother Mary, who was with Mary Magdalene. Before he arrived, Mary stopped, listened and asked: "Why is this night different than every other night?"

Mary Magdalene answered: "Once we were slaves, and we are slaves no longer." The Seder question and answer. The one I had heard many times during Passover at Soni's house.

Mary played her part so movingly, I felt as though I was in her skin as she ran to her son, only to find him being whipped and scourged. The pictures were graphic, as the claws on the scourges tore through her son's flesh. The camera captured the pain on Jesus' face, one bruised and swollen eye shut, and blood pouring from his deep gashes.

And then agony as a crown of thorns was forced down on his head. More blood ran down an already bloodied face. Tears streamed down his mother Mary's face as she beheld her son. Unbidden tears streamed down my face as well as I watched the anguish in Mary's face.

Over and over I watched Mary and Jesus locked together in pain, first in the square and then on the cross. The violence was interlaced with flashbacks of Mary holding her son as a baby, lifting him when his toddling steps could no longer hold him up. I could sense her absolute frustration that this time, she had no power to lift her son. I wept silently as I imagined how I might have felt to have my own son in such pain and to be able to do nothing.

Then scenes of Mary with her son as a carpenter, looking on his work with pride as she made him lunch. The laughing and playful teasing that went on between the two of them made me think of me and my son. I am a mother with a son who was then 22. Not that much younger than Jesus. I connected with Mary and Jesus to the point that I could not speak. Never before had I witnessed such an intense depiction of the relationship between Jesus and his mother.

The whipped and beaten Jesus picked up his cross and dragged it up the hill, often tripping over and falling down on top of it. His mother ran alongside, again trying to get near him. After a horrible slog up Golgotha, Jesus was lashed to the cross and nails were driven through his hands and feet. He screamed. The cross was raised upright and dropped into the waiting hole with a thud. Jesus cried out again. It was more than Mary could take. It was almost more than I could take as well.

Mary rushed to the foot of the cross, her tears bathing her son's bloody feet. Their agony continued unabated for several more minutes. Finally, just before Jesus commended his spirit into his Father's hands, he looked again at his mother. Even at the last, he worried about his mother. Mary expressed a wish to die and go with her son.

With his hair and teeth filled with blood, Jesus gazed down from the cross at his mother's pain-distorted face that was smeared with his blood. He nodded with great difficulty toward John and said, "Mother, behold thy son." And then, "Son, behold thy mother." I wept.

Jesus was dead. A soldier pierced Jesus' side with a sword. Blood and water gushed from his wound. His heart was broken. I was not prepared for how I felt. I was so deeply moved.

Earthquakes and lighting filled the screen. Bricks in the temple fell and crumbled. Soldiers scattered. And then the screen faded to black.

A few moments later, the stone was rolled away from the entrance to the tomb. The funeral linens emptied themselves of their contents. Jesus stood whole. He stepped out of the linens and walked off. Roll credits.

I leaned back in my seat exhausted. I sat in the dark unable to move. I removed my wet and foggy glasses and just let my tears flow freely. Soni looked at me, helplessly. And then the thought came to me: Christ's life wasn't just about his death. The most important event in his life was the resurrection.

"What about the resurrection?" I turned and finally said aloud to Soni. "That's the most important part. The hope of the resurrection."

Then I stopped and didn't know what to make of either my words or my obvious outpouring of emotion. Neither did Soni. We were both amazed at my response. What had happened to my intellectual curiosity? Who was this unbeliever?

As the house lights came up, Soni gently leaned toward me and asked me if I wanted to go somewhere and talk. I nodded yes. I was very shaken.

What was that all about, I wondered? "Pretty interesting behavior for a nonbeliever," I said. Soni thought so as well.

From that night on, Soni tenderly urged me to return to my faith. She could see how much it meant to me, even if I were unwilling to acknowledge it to myself. I finally told her that I was afraid I'd be more judgmental of my own children, who were also inactive, if I ever went back to the Church. I certainly couldn't have been more wrong about that. My love and tenderness for them simply grew after I returned to the Church.

But my comment stopped her in her tracks. At least for the time being. Soni is nothing if not tenacious. And I love that about her. Five years later, when I finally found my way back to my faith, no one was less surprised than my friend Soni.

# PART 3

# A TIME TO HEAL

*For I will restore health unto thee,*
*and I will heal thee of thy wounds.*

—JEREMIAH 30:17

# XII

## Katy and Me

I'd lived in South Orange County for the better part of 17 years, if I didn't count the short 9 months I worked in Hawaii when Alex was in college. I lived there first with my husband and two children. And then with Alex. And then pretty much by myself—or so I thought. I didn't yet know what alone looked like. Alicia was living in Cedar City with Jenna. Alex was finishing his undergraduate work at San Diego State. Norm and Karla had moved to Utah. There was no reason, really, why I couldn't or shouldn't accept the promotion my company was offering me in Sacramento.

I hadn't really moved anywhere for any length of time by myself since college. At that point, at least, most of the people around me were also away from home and in the same boat. This move promised to be far more difficult than that one was. I knew a few people, though not very well, in our Sacramento office. I no longer had the Church to provide me with a ready-made community. And this time, I was taking no one with me.

I spent the first several months in my new job living downtown in a company-paid apartment. I thought I might really enjoy walking to work and being out "where the action was." Sacramento has multiple theatre venues, art museums, historic areas, and fun places to eat. Seemed to be a good plan at the time.

I somehow didn't take into account that it would ostensibly be just me going out to do all these fun things. I found that I didn't feel safe going out alone at night. After dark, the city had its share of pan handlers and homeless people roaming the streets, some of them obviously disturbed. So I wasted most week nights alone, in my one-bedroom apartment with the rented furniture, reading or watching TV.

I literally lived for the weekends, when I would fly home to Orange County. Almost everyone I cared about, and certainly everything I owned but my clothes, was still there. Even Alex was often home for the weekends. I loved hearing him call out as he walked through the door, "Hi Mom!! I'm home." It was so reminiscent of what I still didn't realize was my former life.

I took Alex to dinner, I went to movies and plays with long-standing friends, I enjoyed long walks through tree-lined neighborhoods or down at the harbor by the ocean, and I ate breakfast on my small deck. Or I puttered around my townhome. I rarely read, and I never watched TV.

My weekends were not just the highlight of my life, they were my life. It was hard when Sunday night inevitably rolled around and I had to fly back to Sacramento. After landing, I would make the 15 minute drive downtown to Sacramento, pull into the gated parking lot, and lug my suitcase up the darkened outside steps to the exterior locked, metal door, being cautiously aware of my surroundings. The next day, I started my work week all over again. It wasn't that I didn't enjoy my job. I loved my job, and the people who worked with me. But I had absolutely no life outside of work.

As the weeks passed, I discovered that while I was living my life for the weekends, my friends and Alex were not. I expected, or at least hoped, that since I was so excited to see all of them, they would be just as excited to see me, and would plan their weekends around me. Of course it didn't work out that way. My move had left only a small hole in their lives. But it had left a huge, gaping hole in mine. It was a very difficult time for me, and no one really seemed to completely understand why. Although I told them over and over, until they tired of hearing about it.

I was the one who was starting over again, not them. The space that was my personal life had once been filled with family, friends, and constant activity. The space that was now my personal life was utterly empty. It was clear that I needed to do something. But on most days, I just didn't care. And since I was still commuting home every weekend, it was easy to delay finding new things to fill my time. My life seemed to be shrinking and collapsing in on itself. I was more alone now than I'd ever been. Whose idea was this move? I asked myself. I was frightened and sad.

Predictably, even people who loved me were getting tired of hearing me whine about how I felt. One of my friends, in an effort to help, told me about a single woman she knew who had just moved into her neighborhood. She regaled me with tales of this woman's instant success in making new friends. After living there for only a few months, this "superwoman" apparently had a party in her back yard that was attended by hosts of her new friends. Hearing her story did not help me.

Friends suggested that I join clubs or call the Chamber of Commerce and see what was available in the community. It was probably good advice. But I didn't really feel like doing any of those things. So I just clung to what personal life I had left in Orange County and made everyone around me pretty miserable. It was a terrible way to make no transition at all. I was fortunate to have a good job. It was the only thing preserving my sanity.

Somewhere during my now mostly internal struggles, I got a call from my niece Katy. Her husband Tyler had been applying to law schools. Along with BYU, one of the schools he was considering was McGeorge, which was located right in the heart of downtown Sacramento. I was surprised that they would even consider coming to California. Tyler had been accepted at BYU law school, which was more prestigious and less expensive than McGeorge. As many others in the family did, I asked Katy, "Why McGeorge? Why California?"

"I'm not sure exactly why," she answered. "But we've prayed about it—a lot—and we just know it's the right thing to do." She paused. I was still just listening, surprised. Not surprised that they had prayed about it. That's exactly what they would do. But surprised that they might be coming to Sacramento.

Hearing my silence, Katy went on, "I think Tyler feels as though it would be good for us to spend some time out of Utah, together." She continued, "We thought of Sacramento, because we have family living there." That would be me. Just me.

I was stunned. The reflexive thought that went through my mind at that moment was: I wonder if the Lord is sending Katy and Tyler to Sacramento to bring me back to the Church. I quickly chided myself: What are you thinking? You don't believe in either "the Lord" or the Church.

And then my thoughts immediately morphed into: If those two think they're going to bring me back to the Church, they have another think coming.

Nevertheless, I was ecstatic to think that I might have family moving to Sacramento. Along with my 13 other nieces and nephews, I'd always loved Katy. She is smart, fun, organized, thoughtful, sometimes overly analytical, and always very "fashion forward." Even as a three-year old, she'd been a beautiful, well-dressed—and insistently self-dressed—little girl. I always thought, modestly, that Katy was similar to me in many ways—except for the fashion forward part. I am decidedly tailored and almost never fashion forward.

I didn't know Tyler very well yet, but I liked what I'd seen so far. He was reasoned, but warm. Very responsible and steady. I'd met Tyler's parents when I went to Katy and Tyler's wedding in Salt Lake. I liked them very much. I concluded that Tyler was a great choice for Katy.

After many discussions with their parents, who were often puzzled by Katy and Tyler's eventual decision to move to Sacramento for 3 years, they made the break and came. Katy was pregnant by now and she'd just given up a teaching job that she loved. None of her family and friends (except for Tyler and me) were here either. She was almost as adrift as I was, at least in the beginning. I very much understood how she felt. And I realized that I both needed and wanted to step in and help this growing little family. It felt good to consider looking outside myself, for a change.

For the time Katy lived in the area, we grew to be the best of friends. In August of 2006, cute little Lucy was born, which made things even better. Tyler proved to be a caring and sensitive nephew, who was always considerate of his Aunt Susan. He sometimes invited me to events at McGeorge. And as a one-time "wanna-be" lawyer, I loved listening to the debates. Tyler never failed to give me his signature side-arm hug whenever he said hello or goodbye, in front of his friends or not. And whenever he left my home, he unfailingly added, "We love you, Susan." I knew he meant it. And I loved him right back. He was the soul of patience.

Katy was much more direct with me, particularly about my inactivity in the Church. She was really the only one who was. I was determined to tolerate her comments and questions about my feelings for the Church; much as a big momma dog might tolerate an earnest little puppy. I hadn't counted on how determined she would actually be.

"My dad says you still know the Church is true," she announced one day, when we were driving somewhere together in the car, and I had no means of escape.

Her words astonished me. What was my brother Brent thinking? Was he kidding? Did he not know how far I'd drifted away? Could he not see that I was never coming back?

I tried to reply to Katy as kindly and patiently as I could. I knew how important the Church was to her. "You know how much I love your dad, Katy. And you know how much I love you. But I'm afraid he's wrong. I don't know that the Church is true anymore."

Katy pressed on, "Do you mean to tell me that you don't believe in the Book of Mormon anymore, or in Joseph Smith either?"

How to put this to her gently. "I'm afraid I don't, Katy." That made her sad. This in turn made me sad. But it was what it was. Katy gave it up for that day. But there would be other days.

The Church wasn't the only thing Katy and I talked about. But since the Church was a very essential something in Katy's life, she refused to exclude it from our conversations. That was fine with me, as long as I didn't have to believe it was true.

Katy, Tyler, and I spent many hours together, eating out or watching movies in. If I had still been using the word blessing, I would have said that Katy and Tyler were a huge blessing in my life. They made my transition to a full-fledged empty nester much easier. I eventually flew home less and less, partly out of financial necessity, and partly because I had family here in Sacramento.

In the last analysis, starting all over again in a new place proved to be exactly what I needed to do. Leaving at least some people and places behind allowed me to make a clean break with what wasn't always stellar behavior on my part. It was much easier to break undesirable habits out of familiar environments.

I needed the chance to reinvent myself. Moving to Sacramento was the catalyst that gave me that opportunity, although I certainly did not see, or appreciate it, at the time. Having Katy there with me made all the difference. It was Katy and Tyler's love for me that jump-started the healing in my life, and my eventual return to the Church.

# XIII

# And a Little Child Shall Lead Them

O ur Jenna had just turned 8 years old. It was hard for me to believe that 8 years of her life had whizzed past us so quickly. What happened to the little three-year old girl who loved jumping on the trampoline in Dave's back yard? The one who reported happily that her head didn't even hit the sky? The same little Jenna who liked to swing in swings and sing the song, "Small World"?

It was even harder to believe that it was the same Jenna who had decided all on her own that she wanted to be baptized a member of the Church. That was really a big-girl decision. It had been quite some time since Alicia and Jenna had attended church with any degree of regularity. I certainly wasn't active, and neither was Alex.

Even today, none of us is quite certain what prompted Jenna to make the decision to be baptized. Not even Jenna. But prompted she was. Jenna decided that being baptized was important to her, and she wasn't going to let anything stand in her way of making it happen.

Alicia asked Jenna several times if she were sure she wanted to be baptized. Jenna always said yes, she was sure she wanted to be baptized. So Alicia finally took Jenna in to meet with the bishop. I imagine he might have been a little surprised, when this small, inactive little 8-year old girl, who was almost swallowed up in the big chair in his office, sat up as tall as she could and announced with certainty that she wanted to be baptized. In the eyes of the Church, Jenna had reached the age of accountability. She was 8-years old and was old enough to make this decision with her mother's consent.

Alicia was supportive of whatever Jenna wanted to do. The bishop told Jenna that before she could be baptized, she needed to attend Primary for at least 2 months, probably so she could be confident in the decision she was making. And likely so he could also see that she was really willing to make the commitment to be baptized.

Jenna readily agreed to the bishop's conditions, and Alicia started taking her to church. Two months is a long time in the life of an 8-year old. But Jenna faithfully attended church every week and listened to her Primary teachers tell her what it meant to be baptized a member of the Church and to receive the Holy Ghost.

Not surprisingly, Jenna asked her Uncle Dave to baptize her. He and Jaci had been a constant in her life since she was born, and she loved them both. They were happy to make the trip from Salt Lake to Cedar City to participate in Jenna's baptism. And since this was obviously something that was very important to Jenna, Alex and I promised to make the trip from California as well. Jenna asked her Grandpa Swann to confirm her. So it seemed that our splintered little family would be together again, if just for the day.

When Alex and I rolled in to Cedar City, Dave and Jaci weren't long behind us. We all checked in, changed into our Sunday best, and drove over to the Church. Jenna bounced over to meet us as we came through the door. She was absolutely beautiful all dressed up in a pink dress, dotted with pink roses and framed with pink ribbons—a veritable picture in pink. Her blonde hair was cut short in a little pixie cut. She was thrilled that her whole family had come for her special day.

Jenna and Dave went to get dressed in their white baptismal clothes. I waited for them in the foyer, while Alicia went to help Jenna. After they were ready, I asked Jenna to sit down on her Uncle Dave's lap, so I could take their picture. She sat expectantly, dressed in her long, white jumpsuit, a broad and slightly toothless grin spreading across her radiant little face, eyes beaming. Dave held Jenna confidently on his lap, close to his heart, as I snapped their photo. They made a lovely picture, the two of them sitting there together: My all-grown-up handsome baby brother with a family of his own, holding my precious granddaughter Jenna on his lap.

If I hadn't still been so focused on what I yet lacked in my life, my heart would have swelled with gratitude at watching Dave and Jenna sitting there together. But I was still wasting energy grieving for what was gone, rather than finding love and strength in the wonderful people and events that still remained. Precious time lost, never to be regained.

I turned to my Alicia who was standing next to me and said, "You're a wonderful mother, sweetheart. You take good care of Jenna. I know you go without to give her what she needs. I'm very proud of you."

"Thanks, Mom," Alicia responded, her eyes filling. And then mine did too.

"Are you guys crying?" Jenna asked, as she slid off of Dave's lap. "Why are you crying?"

"We're just happy," I said.

"I don't know why you two cry when you're happy," Jenna said.

"We just do sometimes," Alicia responded, bending down and hugging Jenna. We left Jenna with Dave and walked to the chapel.

As I walked in with Alicia, I saw my ex-husband sitting next to his wife. It still surprises me a little when I see them together. I did believe that, on the day I had left, I had moved on with my life. And that I had done so years ago. I didn't fully realize then that I'd gotten stuck somewhere along the way. Financially, I had moved on. But in other ways, maybe not so much. My anger and "my story of loss," still kept me tied to a marriage that had long since disintegrated. I had not yet found forgiveness in my heart.

We all took our seats in the chapel, waiting for the children who would be baptized to join us. I sat on the bench next to Alicia and Jaci. Alex sat just ahead of us, and my ex and his wife were on the bench in front of Alex. It all felt a little awkward to me. But as my former husband and I exchanged friendly greetings, and even shared a few laughs, I so clearly remember the way my son Alex kept looking back and forth from one of us to the other, his face so obviously registering happiness and amazement that his parents were so engaged in amicable conversation. Alicia had a look of pleasant surprise on her face as well, as she looked down the row.

As I watched my children watch us, I was filled with such a deep sense of sadness and regret that we hadn't done a better job of being co-parents. I'd heard of people who had. One of my former co-workers and her ex-husband spoke civilly and regularly. They spent holidays together with their children and new spouses. They were selfless enough to know that it was all about their children—and not about any residual, hostile feelings they still harbored for each other.

I so wished at that moment that I'd been mature enough to set aside my acrimony and sense of injustice for the benefit of my children. That day, as I looked into their happy faces, I could see just how important it was to them that their parents got along, even if it was just for a few hours.

I watched then as our sweet little Jenna came through the door of the chapel and walked down to the front row, her proud, Great-Uncle Dave sheparding her in and helping her find her seat on the bench. I could see the look of excitement and anticipation on Jenna's face as she waved to her family and sat down next to the other children.

Jenna listened quietly and carefully to each of the speakers, who talked about what an important day this was in her life and the lives of each of the other children and their families. I could see the intent look on Jenna's face as she tried to understand and mentally record the importance of the step she was taking by being baptized a member of her family's church.

After the talks ended, and we sang the closing song and listened to the closing prayer, we moved into the room next to the baptismal font. When it was Jenna's turn to be baptized, Dave led her carefully down the steps and into the waist-deep water. We all moved to the front row to be as close to Jenna as we could. She looked up from the water and smiled at all of us. And waved again. She was so happy to see us all here together, just for her.

Dave repeated his last-minute instructions, telling Jenna to hold her nose and bend her knees. Then he tenderly placed his foot right next to hers, so her feet wouldn't fly up when she went under the water. Jenna put one hand on Dave's arm and held her nose with the other. She closed her eyes as Dave raised his arm to the square and repeated the words of the baptismal ordinance. Then he gently laid her all the way under the water, as Jenna's hair spread out in wet wisps around her head. And then he brought her quickly back up.

Jenna came up sputtering, wiping the water out of her eyes, smiling joyously. Jenna was a very little girl, who had made a very big decision, all by herself. She had set a goal, met the Bishop's requirements, gathered her family together, and been baptized. Jenna was now officially a member of the Church of Jesus Christ of Latter-day Saints, similar to all the other members of her family. We were all proud of our little girl.

Alicia stood ready with a big, fluffy towel. She bundled Jenna in it and hurried her to the rest room to change out of her wet clothes. Jaci was there with a towel for Dave, as he climbed the steps out of the font, dripping wet from the waist down. I mouthed the words "Thank you," to my brother. He smiled his familiar, steady, even smile, and nodded back at me.

After Jenna and Dave were dressed, Jenna's grandpa confirmed her. I don't remember much about what he said when he confirmed her. I do know that he conferred the Holy Ghost on her and blessed Jenna that His Spirit would always be with her to direct her and guide her along her life's path.

I wish I could say that I was spiritually moved by this important event in my Jenna's life. I wish I could say that I felt the same sense of love and joy that Jenna felt that night. I wish I could say that I felt a sense of forgiveness and being forgiven. But I felt none of those things. Not yet.

Tonight I could only be touched somewhere deep inside me by the example of my little Jenna, who was filled with such faith and such a sense of pure love for everyone in her family. She knew and understood much more than I did about the importance of making and keeping commitments and being led by the Spirit to help her make important decisions.

"... And a little child shall lead them." Isaiah 11:6.

# XIV

# El Dorado Hills

It was by now the summer of 2006. I was living in Davis, California, in an apartment west of Sacramento. Davis itself is a fine place:
small, college-town, eclectic shops, and up-scale restaurants. But it still
didn't feel like home. And I didn't really like my apartment. The apartment itself was nice enough: 2 bedrooms, double garage, nice location.
But it was noisy. Really noisy, in my opinion.

Above my bedroom lived a couple of college students who liked to
party late—this was, after all, a college town. Above my living room lived
a small family with a 3-year old boy with black, straight hair. He was a
handsome little boy with a happy smile, who delighted in jumping off of
beds, chairs, couches, or just jumping on the floor above me for the sheer
joy of it. Good for him, bad for me, I thought, as he thundered regularly
across my ceiling.

I wanted to buy a house. But I was worried that the real estate market
was shaky and showing signs of fraying. I'd looked at a place in Davis. I
even put money down on a small condo for a few hours, before reneging
on the deal. My agent assured me that the value of real estate in Davis was
strong and would never drop. I wasn't so sure. And it just didn't feel right.
So I decided to just wait and watch.

A few weeks later, I was sitting in my living room reading the Sunday paper and listening to the joys of jumping overhead. As usual, I was
pouring over the real estate ads. I came across an ad that caught my eye:
Bonus homes in El Dorado Hills. I wasn't certain what was meant by
bonus homes, but it sounded promising and the price was great. The devel-
oper was also offering free upgrades. I was intrigued.

My friend Carole's sister had lived in El Dorado Hills. I'd been to her home once. I remembered the area as a lovely place in the hills not too far east of Sacramento. Far enough out of Sacramento that I didn't need to be concerned about the aging levees surrounding the city. I decided to drive out to El Dorado Hills and have a look. Couldn't hurt.

I pulled a cold bottle of water out of the fridge, grabbed my purse and a light jacket for protection against the chilling fall weather, and got in my car. I soon found myself passing a sign on the freeway that read: South Lake Tahoe. Now that sounded good! I'd been to Lake Tahoe a few times and especially loved the hot air balloon ride I'd taken over the lake.

It took me another 30 minutes to reach El Dorado Hills. Not a terrible commute from Sacramento, I noted. A stone sign announced El Dorado Hills, followed by a green sign that read: Population 34,000. I liked that number. As much as I'd wanted to leave the small town where I'd grown up, at this point in my life, I was very drawn again to small towns. I turned off the exit and passed the El Dorado Hills Town Center, an attractive, tree-lined boulevard with lots of boutique shops and a large cinema at the end of the street. I loved the small-town feel of it. The easy pace of the place.

I soon drove through the open gate of the development and parked my car in the lot opposite the sales office. I got out and paused for a moment as I took note of gently rolling hills mounding in the distance. I took a deep gulp of fresh foothill air and then crossed the street.

I opened the door to the sales office. A saleswoman whose name tag read "Nancy" approached me. She looked to be somewhere in her early sixties. Blondish hair, nice smile. "May I help you"? She asked.

"I'm here about the bonus homes."

"Ah, yes. You must have seen the ad we ran in today's *Sac Bee*."

"I did. Yes. What exactly do you mean by "bonus homes?"

"Please come into my office," Nancy said, closing the door behind us as we sat down. "We have about 6 bonus homes in the area. We're offering them for a steal, which includes upgrades such as granite counter tops and 5" baseboards."

"Why are you dropping the price now?" I inquired.

"We're moving into the last quarter of the year," Nancy continued.

"We're a publicly traded company. We have sales numbers we need to make before the end of the year. Keep the analysts happy, you know."

Made sense to me.

"The thing to know about the bonus homes is that they have to be sold with no contingencies. If you make an offer, it can't be subject to the sale of your home. And you have to be ready and able to close before the end of the year," Nancy said, outlining the conditions.

My town home in Aliso Viejo was rented. Who knew if that had been a good idea? If the market dropped too far, I'd lose money. If the market eventually came back, I'd be ok. I had decided to take the risk and not sell my place in Aliso—and I was pretty sure I could get out of my short-term apartment lease in Davis. There were always students looking for an apartment to rent in a college town.

"Not a problem," I replied. "I can close before the end of the year."

"Excellent!" Nancy grinned broadly, smelling the prospect of a sale. "Shall we take a look?"

"Why not?" I answered her.

We walked out the door of the office into the crisp sunshine. I could see hints of fall colors here and there in some of the trees and bushes. We eventually found ourselves inside a home called the Lake Tahoe. I loved the high ceilings in this floor plan, which made it seem even more open. There were side lights framing the entry way and lots of big windows throughout the house, filling it with natural light.

The kitchen had cherry wood cabinets, stainless steel appliances, a breakfast nook, and a large island in the middle of the floor. The kitchen also opened into the great room, which had a family room/dining room combination and a fireplace on one end. The mantle on the fireplace looked similar to the mantle on the fireplace in the home where I'd grown up.

The master bedroom and bathroom were spacious, with a huge walk-in closet. There was no way that my clothes would ever fill that closet. But it would be fun to try. And I loved the idea of such a big closet, after the generally cramped closets I'd been living with for the past 11 years. It amazed me to think that I might actually be able to afford a place such as this.

The backyard was private and unfinished. Just dirt and a high fenced retaining wall. There was a covered patio that I could extend if I wanted to and a good-sized side yard. I hadn't had a yard in what seemed like forever. I could plant grass, flowers, and fruit frees. A real yard!

"Why don't we go take a look at the community lodge?" Nancy offered. "It's just around the corner on the next street over." So we walked around the block to the lodge. We walked through the parking lot, past the tall, bubbling water fountain, and alongside the riot of colored flowers bordering the lodge.

The lodge itself is a large stone mason and stucco building. It has a good-sized ballroom for parties, a full kitchen with commercial appliances, a library, and a craft room (Not for me. I had never been particularly good at crafts), a small movie room, card rooms, and a fitness center replete with both women's and men's lockers and restrooms. It was nicely appointed and looked very inviting.

"This is lovely," I said appreciatively. So much for not looking too eager.

"Wait until you see the pool and tennis courts," Nancy smiled, holding the back door open for me. Sure enough, sprawling out in front of me, sat a large L-shaped swimming pool that went anywhere from 3 feet to 5 feet deep. Deep enough to dive in, I thought, even though there were posted signs that discouraged diving. There were brown chaise lounges, chairs, tables with glass table tops, and big umbrellas surrounding the pool. I could see a few happy couples chatting in the hot tub, which was off to the side of the pool. It looked like a resort.

Nancy and I walked through the pool area to the tennis courts and then up the steps to a large barbecue area with a bocce ball court. I'd played tennis on my high school tennis team as a sophomore and then played for fun in college. I might take up the game again, I mused, as Nancy told me a bit about the women's and men's tennis teams who played at least weekly.

After we left the lodge, we took a short walk along one of the many walking trails that criss-crossed through the community. The trails themselves were paved, but the areas on the sides of the trails had been left natural with river grasses, cat tails, and tall trees or planted with flowers. I saw red-winged black birds clustering in one large oak tree. It was quiet. It was peaceful. I could walk, I could swim, and I could play tennis. Something inside me whispered, this is it. Buy this place. Move here.

Was it possible that I could actually afford to live in this place? I ran the numbers in my head, as I had done many times on paper. I could swing it. But what if this isn't the bottom of the market? I asked myself. What if the price drops even further? I knew that it might. But if I wait much longer, the relocation package will expire. And how long will it be possible to get these kinds of loans? The debate continued inside my head. When you know it's the bottom of the market, it's already too late. Take a chance. It feels right.

"Let's go back to your office, Nancy. I'd like to make an offer," I finally said. Which Nancy was more than happy to do.

After we got back to the sales office, I went into the design center and selected granite counter tops for the kitchen and bathrooms. The granite in the kitchen had bits of glittering iron pyrite embedded in the stone. I added dark brown, iron-looking lighting features to my otherwise modern home. My choices seemed appropriate, given the mining history of the area. I knew that a twenty minute drive or so up Highway 50 stood Sutter's Mill, where gold was first discovered in California. I liked being close to that piece of history.

What I didn't know until later was that on the site of Sutter's Mill stood Mormon cabin, which had housed former members of the Mormon battalion, who originally camped along the American River before coming to Sutter's Mill looking for work. A few hours away from Sutter's Mill, toward the western edge of what is now Tahoe National Forest, runs Pioneer Trail, where many other Mormons crossed emigrant trails in the area to travel into California, following the discovery of gold.

About 8 miles away from my new home was more Mormon history, evidenced by the remnants of Mormon Island, which in its heyday was a thriving gold mining camp, whose 2,500 residents were mostly Mormon. While the old town was flooded in 1955 when Folsom Lake was created, the green sign that announces "Mormon Island" still stands.

Ten miles down the hill in Folsom, overlooking Lake Natoma, is the new Sacramento temple, which had been dedicated just the month prior to my coming to El Dorado Hills to look at real estate. Katy and Tyler had taken me through the Sacramento Temple open house, but being the geographically challenged person I am, I had not thought about the proximity of the temple to my potentially new home in El Dorado Hills. It seemed that I had planned to move to an area where I was surrounded on all sides by my Mormon heritage. I was quite unaware and unappreciative of it all until much later. This area would prove to have lots of strong members of my church.

A few days after meeting with Nancy and submitting my offer, my offer was accepted. A few weeks after that, I got the loan. Less than 2 months later, I moved into my new house, with a lot of help from Alex, Katy, and Tyler. Little Lucy slept in her car seat in the master closet while we worked to bring in the furniture and unpack the boxes. A few weeks later, the new blinds finally showed up. It felt like home.

I loved the peace and calm of living in the Foothills. Sunsets filled the evening skies with pink and purple flower buds that changed into brilliant points of light in the darkened night sky. Days dawned on quiet feet, accompanied by the sound of cooing mourning doves. I passed horses and cows grazing in green pastures and watched sunshine skate over meadows as I drove down side roads for my morning commute. When I came home in the early evening, as I crested the hill that dropped down into our little community, it looked similar to the mythical city of Brigadoon off in the distance. I think I was half afraid that I might come home one night and find that it had completely disappeared.

In the summer, I swam laps in the pool and then lay on a chaise in the warm California sun. Or I played a game of tennis with the ladies or talked with my neighbors over the fence. My neighbors were the best ever. Bob came over when something needed to be repaired. Mimi watched my home when I was out of town. We had block parties and progressive dinners or a friendly game of bocce ball.

In the fall, I drove to Apple Hill and bought apples, homemade caramel, and fresh apple pie. I went for long walks down the trails, past brilliant fall colors, waving to friends as I passed. When the winter rains came, I curled up nights in front of the fire and read a book. My home became my sanctuary. And my healing began in earnest.

# XV

# The Church Finds Me Again

*M*y home phone was ringing. I didn't recognize the name on the display. Someone named Val. Last name Stevens. "Hello?" I answered, my voice rising into more of a question than a statement. Who was this guy and what did he want?

"Is this Susan Swann?" came the voice on the other end.

"It is," I replied. "Is this a sales call? Because if it is, I don't accept sales calls." That was what I always said when people I didn't know called me around dinner time.

"No. This is Val Stevens from the El Dorado Hills ward. We live here in your neighborhood. Just a few blocks away from you."

"Oh . . . hello," I said a bit more warmly. Church members and neighbors both. I hope he doesn't think that I want to come back to church.

Just weeks before Val's call, Merrill Hales, the ward high priest group leader, came to pay me a visit. He and his counselor were very nice people. And I enjoyed meeting them. Then as expected, Merrill got around to inviting me back to church. I declined, as I had so many times over the past 14 years. "I'm not interested. But I appreciate you coming by," I said, as I ushered them out the door.

And now another attempt from the Church to contact me. This time from someone named Val Stevens. Home teacher, perhaps? The Church had lost track of me for awhile. I'd lived at a few different addresses in the Sacramento area before buying my home in El Dorado Hills. And I didn't exactly provide the Church with a forwarding address.

I'd lived in El Dorado Hills now for about 14 months, so it had taken the Church a while to find me. But the Church is relentlessly caring and concerned about its members. So I wasn't that surprised to hear from them again.

Val continued. "My wife Dorothy and I are your home teachers."

Bingo.

"We wondered if we might come by and see you sometime this week."

I had never turned down visits from home teachers, I reminded myself. If I were so "done with the Church," I wondered, why not? Didn't matter. A part of me liked having them come.

"I'll be out of town all week on business," I responded. "But we could make it next week, if you like."

"How about next Wednesday night?" Val asked.

I quickly consulted my day planner. "That works."

"What's a good time for you?"

"How about 7:00 p.m.?"

"Sounds good. Dorothy and I will see you then. We're looking forward to meeting you."

"Me too," I hoped. He sounded nice enough. "Bye."

The next Wednesday, promptly at 7:00, my doorbell rang. Here we go, I thought. I walked to my front door and glanced quickly through the peep hole. There stood a man and his wife about my age. She was holding a flower. Nice gesture, I thought. He was about 6' tall, silver gray hair, wearing a pair of sports pants and a collared shirt. Warm eyes. She looked to be about 5'8," thin, blonde, shoulder-length hair, and wearing a yellow blouse with matching sandals. An attractive couple. They looked harmless enough.

I opened the door. "Hello," I said. "Come in, please." I led them down the hall past my study and into the great room. I invited them to sit opposite me on the tan, L-shaped couch that sits in the middle of the room.

"I love your couch," Dorothy commented. "It's so soft and deep. And the back is high. It's very comfortable."

I smiled. "Thanks. I like it. My son talked me into buying it. He's about 6'7" so a deep couch with a high back was essential for him. He was sorry to see it go when I moved it here."

"Wow! 6'7," Val commented. "Now that's tall. Is he a basketball player?"

I always got that question when people found out how tall Alex was. I guess it's hard to imagine a male that tall who doesn't play basketball. "He was," I answered. "High school center. Until he tore his meniscus. That pretty much ended his basketball career."

"That's too bad," Val replied, concerned.

"It's really ok," I said. "I think it bothered me more than it did him. He really prefers surfing or snowboarding."

"Does he live in the area?" Val asked.

"No. He lives in Southern California. My daughter and grand-daughter live in St. George." Then the Stevens asked to see pictures of my family, which I was more than happy to share with them.

We talked for an hour or so. Val mentioned that he had graduated from McGeorge Law School. I told him Tyler was attending McGeorge. Something in common. Val and Dorothy both smiled a lot and laughed easily. They listened more than they talked. A rare quality in anyone, I thought. I was happy to have a husband and wife team as my home teachers. They were just right for me, and they were not put off when I expressed a lack of interest in the Church.

Over the next few months, Val and Dorothy came to see me regularly. They rarely came empty handed: a loaf of bread, a jar of jam, a plant, a tea towel. They always called before coming. They didn't give up when I resisted their invitations to come to church, but they didn't push me either. Our conversations were interesting. We mostly got to know each other better.

Val and Dorothy always wanted to end our visit with prayer. That was fine with me, as long as I didn't have to say it. Since it was my home, Val always asked me who I wanted to say the prayer. I never picked me. But still I appreciated, on some level, their prayers on my behalf.

During one of their visits, after they felt comfortable with me, they gently inquired as to why I had left the Church. They listened attentively and without judgment or interruption as I told them my story. I think everyone who leaves the Church has a story. And I think most of us want to share it with someone. As my new friends listened, their gentle spirits of concern touched me. Regardless of how I felt about my membership in the Church at this juncture, I appreciated the Stevens' friendship.

Certainly I'd been invited back to church many times. Family, neighbors, friends, home teachers, and worried bishops had all extended the invitation over the past several years. I'd like to think that I was always gracious—albeit firm—in my refusal to go back to church. I had tried going to a Mormon church once in Davis. I hadn't felt at all comfortable in the meeting that day. Too conservative for my tastes, I reasoned.

So I visited a Unitarian church. Very nice people. You could pretty much believe anything you wanted to and be a Unitarian. A bit too liberal for me, though. So I tried a Presbyterian church. Perhaps something in the middle? Very friendly and inclusive, I thought, but the rituals didn't feel familiar. And while the pastors gave good sermons, I missed having a lay ministry, where most of the congregation was fairly skilled at delivering a message. No. It was my church or none at all. And since I didn't believe in either God or my own church, it was none at all.

I did go to church with my mom when I visited her. Or my brothers when I visited them. Or when any of them visited me. And while I respected their beliefs, I didn't believe a word of it anymore.

I told Val and Dorothy that I might consider coming to church one day when the new chapel was built. Val and Dorothy generously offered me a ride to church. "No," I said. "Thank you." I wasn't sure if I'd really go, or if I did, how long I'd be willing to stay.

Once the chapel on Scholar Way was completed, I went to one sacrament meeting. I'd driven past the new church a few times, so I knew where it was. I loved the fact that the chapel sat on a street called "Scholar Way," right across from a junior college. I really did try to enjoy being at church that day. But I couldn't agree with many of the ideas that were expressed. The congregation seemed to be filled with nice people, so I was sorry I didn't like being there.

Not long after that, Val called and invited me to their home for dinner. It seemed that our community had a family home evening group they called, appropriately enough, the empty nesters. This particular month, it was Val and Dorothy's turn to host. I agreed, somewhat reluctantly. This might be kind of strange, I thought. But it was Val and Dorothy who had asked me, so I decided to go.

I arrived at the Stevens' door the next Monday. I was nervous. I was inactive. How would the others feel about me? How would I feel about them? But I was here . . . standing at their door . . . so I knocked. Softly.

Val opened the door with a big grin. Dorothy waved hello from the kitchen. They had a lovely home. And the food smelled good. Val took me inside and introduced me to the other empty nesters. They were friendly. I'm not sure they knew quite what to do with me at first. Who is this woman? I think they wondered.

As we gathered around the tables for dinner, Val sat next to me and smiled encouragingly. Dorothy made every effort to be inclusive. I could sense their love and support for me. And I appreciated it. I appreciated them.

After we finished dessert, Val asked us to move our chairs into a circle for the short family home evening lesson. I hadn't counted on that part. But it was too late to leave now. Val had opted for a simple lesson that night. One in which I could easily participate. And one that took me back to another place and time in my relationship with the Church.

The topic was: Relate an event you remember from your days in Primary. There were some very funny stories. We all laughed together as we recalled things we'd said and done as children. It was a very easy time we spent together that night. I felt part of the group.

As I tried to think about what to share, childhood memories of Primary came back to me that I hadn't thought about in years. They were happy, warm memories of simple stories, familiar songs, and even Primary parades, where I proudly rode my blue Schwinn bike with multicolored streamers coming from the handle bars, next to my brother Norm. I recalled green bandalos, ice cream parties, and making little dioramas with Nephite warriors. But which memory to share with the group?

In the end, I decided to tell my new friends just how much I'd loved getting gold stars on my forehead in Primary, when I was 3-years old. I told them I'd been so taken with the idea of getting a gold star that I asked every week to be allowed to get up and recite a nursery rhyme, along with the other children who were actually giving assigned talks.

It turned out to be a pretty revealing story, I'm afraid. But the empty nesters took it in stride and with humor. They were very kind. No hidden agendas. I let down my guard. I felt safe with them. They expected nothing from me. They gave me only friendship in return.

It got to the point where I wanted to take my turn as hostess. I think they were surprised. But they happily agreed. So one Monday night, the empty nesters came to my house. It had been forever since I'd had either the desire or the where-with-all to entertain comfortably. But now I did.

As I gathered the group together in a circle after we finished eating, I'm sure they all wondered what I was going to do for a lesson. I was, after all, still an inactive non-believer.

I kept it light. I asked them to share someone or something they were grateful for. The only rule was that no one could be grateful for the same thing someone else had already used. I didn't want them all to say they were grateful for their families or their testimonies of the Church. They agreed to the ground rules, and we started around the circle.

When we got to Val, he said he was grateful for Dorothy and her willingness to marry him, even though Dorothy's father apparently had some serious reservations about Val, when his car broke down on a trip he and Dorothy took from Utah to California. What kind of man, after all, doesn't keep his car in good repair at all times? We all found that part of his story pretty funny.

When we got to Mike, he said, "So, if I understand the rules, I can't be grateful for Dorothy. Is that right?" That got a good laugh from all of us.

When it came to my turn, I picked my career to be grateful for, since family and friends had already been used. The others asked me lots of questions. Curious, caring questions. Not intrusive kinds of questions. They wanted to know where I'd come from and how and why I'd ended up moving to El Dorado Hills.

It was an emotional moment for me as I gave them the "Reader's Digest" version of my story. I could feel their empathy for my losses. I could feel their pride in my turn around. They understood me better. They appreciated how difficult life had once been for me and my children, and they were happy to have me here with them now.

I sensed their warmth and acceptance. I could feel myself begin to break free from the story that had held me captive and come to define me too narrowly for too long. It was yesterday's news. So I started to let go of it.

Right around that time, I became more interested in reading religious philosophers again—although not LDS writers. I generally focused on ancient Chinese philosophers. I liked the gentleness and stillness of their beliefs. And I also started listening to Church hymns. I was somehow drawn to them, although I had no idea why. I bought a CD of the Mormon Tabernacle Choir and listened to hymns in my car as I drove home from work. I loved singing along with songs such as, "Abide with Me" or "Now the Day is Over." Or "Lead Kindly Light."

A friend of mine who was also inactive asked me why I listened to the hymns. Was I a believer? I told her no. I wasn't. I just enjoyed listening. Neither one of us understood my answer. But it didn't matter. I still liked listening to the hymns.

I started thinking that there must be more to life than just working, entertaining myself, or watching over my children from afar. My career was stable. I had more than I needed financially. My family seemed to be doing fine, and my children no longer really needed me in their lives in the same way they had when they were younger.

I'd spent a lot of time over the last 14 years just surviving. Since my survival now seemed relatively assured, I started wondering, who is Susan? It would take me a few years more to find an answer to that question. But I continued looking. And I found myself increasingly drawn to my community of faith.

# XVI
# Doctor Walt

*I*t was by now early July of 2008, and I was spending a few days in Twin Falls with my mom. The dedication of the Twin Falls temple was on approach, and it was the primary topic of conversation at both my mom's house and my brother Brent's.

Brent was the chairman of the Twin Falls temple committee. He was highly invested in the construction and dedication of the temple and had been since it was announced 2 years ago. My niece Annie was the official temple photographer. My nephew Dave was practicing for the cultural celebration scheduled to be performed the night before the dedication. In fact, everyone here in my family was involved with the temple project in some way or another. Their enthusiasm was so pervasive, I could almost touch it.

Brent had been asked to speak at the ground-breaking ceremony two years earlier. He asked me now if I'd be interested in watching the DVD of the ceremony. I was still resisting all things religious, but I was so proud of Brent. I always had been, ever since he was a little boy with his wide toothless grin and beaming brown eyes. If this was important to him, then it was important to me.

As Brent slid the DVD into the player, I settled back comfortably in the large leather recliner in his living room and flipped up the foot rest. I had to admit that it was generally hard for me to participate in these kinds of events. They usually made me feel uncomfortable in some way and served to separate me from others who were engaged in ways that I was not. And I could usually read the anxious looks on my family's faces as they hoped something would touch me in ways that I couldn't imagine.

As the pictures of the temple ground-breaking pulsed across the screen, I heard Brent's timbered voice rise through the speakers. He'd always been an excellent speaker, able to reach the hearts of those who were within the sound of his voice. This talk was absolutely no exception.

The words Brent said that I remember most came at the point when he spoke about "standing on the shoulders of giants." He spoke about the early pioneers who first settled this area and its surrounding valleys. He made reference to our great-grandfather, Horton David Haight, who'd been asked by Brigham Young to move his family away from Farmington, Utah, to settle in Oakley, Idaho.

It couldn't have been easy to be asked to move yet again, I thought. And while my great-grandmother went with him willingly, I understand that she cried all the way to Oakley. On November 19, 1887, the Cassia stake was organized. Elder Haight was called to be its first president.

Brent had also served as a stake president in the Twin Falls West Stake. I thought how proud his ancestors would be of him if they could see him now, breaking ground for a new temple. He'd worked hard to unite the surrounding communities in making this temple their own.

Then the thought came to me: I wonder if my ancestors are proud of me too? I hoped that in some way they were. But I was even more certain that in other ways they weren't. That thought caused me no small degree of sadness. I brushed away a tear from the corner of my eye.

As Brent's talk concluded, I thanked him for sharing the DVD with me and told him that his talk was stirring. Which it was. But I had had enough. "They might need my help in the kitchen," I said aloud, as I rose from my chair and walked quickly across the floor to join the others, who were debating about what to feed the growing crowd. I set aside my contradictory feelings for the time being and searched for a cookie. Or maybe two.

Later that night, back at my mother's, I lay in bed enjoying the quiet, listening to the old grandfather clock tick tocking softly out in the living room. I'd loved that clock when it stood in the hall of my Grandfather Hatch's home in Burley when I was growing up. Then I remembered that my Grandfather Hatch had also served as a stake president in the area. He too would have been proud of Brent. It seemed that I was hemmed in by the ghosts of family members past.

Why did it matter, I wondered, whether or not my ancestors were proud of me? I was only speaking conceptually, of course. Since all life ended with death, they weren't really thinking anything. So what did it matter anyway? But I was unable to stop the tears that were now flowing freely. On some level my feelings made no sense to me at all. It shouldn't matter what ancestors thought who no longer existed. But it did matter, I had to admit. And more than a little.

There was something about building a temple in an area where I had spent my childhood, and where my dad, mother, grandparents on both sides, and even great-grandparents had spent their lives as well. This all resonated with me in ways that I couldn't explain. I couldn't be here for the upcoming temple open house. But I was here now. I decided that I'd ask Brent if it would be possible for me to walk through the temple with him tomorrow. I knew that visiting the temple would leave me open to even more messy feelings. But I needed to go through anyway.

The next morning arrived filled with Idaho sunshine and fluffy white clouds that scudded across blue skies. I called Brent's house to ask if he could take me on a tour of the temple. Marcia told me that a few volunteers from stakes throughout the area, who would eventually staff the open house, were being trained today in the temple. Brent was going over and she thought that I could go with him. She seemed a little surprised by my request and reminded me that I would need to wear a dress. My typical attire was pants suits.

I assured her that I would find something appropriate to wear. I'd brought a black skirt with me, but I decided that it was probably too short for this particular occasion. My mom offered to help me find something more suitable to wear. So into her closets we ventured, looking for just the right thing.

We eventually settled on a reddish dress, mid-calf length, with a black collar and cuffs. I tried it on. It was the right size, so in that sense it fit me. It didn't look similar to anything I would ever wear, however. My mom and I both laughed at my reflection in the full-length mirror. "You don't look like yourself," she smiled. She was right.

"I don't feel life myself, Mom," I answered. But the dress didn't look terrible on me, so I decided to wear it anyway. It was bad enough that Brent had an inactive sister. At least I didn't have to dress like one.

Brent soon pulled up out front. He also smiled just a little when he saw me. "Is that Mom's dress," he asked?

"It is," I replied. "And it's probably better than my short black skirt." No argument there, although I think he would have been fine no matter what I wore.

I found my anxiety rising slightly as we approached the temple grounds. What would today be like for me? Brent pulled into the parking lot of the new one-story meeting house that stood near the temple. We got out of the car and crossed the parking lot. I noticed that someone had scrawled obscene anti-Mormon graffiti in pink chalk on the sidewalk.

Brent seemed to take it in stride. This wasn't the first problem they'd had. But I found myself angry. Whatever happened to civil disagreement? Did people regularly deface the sidewalks of Catholic or Baptist churches when they were constructed? I thought not.

Brent told me that the temple had attracted its share of out-of-the-area paid protestors, who you would otherwise know in a small town like Twin Falls. These folks had been picketing and brandishing anti-Mormon signs, while Mormon Church members crossed the street, offered them cold water and the occasional cookie when the days got long and hot.

While I reminded myself that I was now neither Mormon nor Christian, these were still my people. It wasn't in my heart to tolerate less than charitable behavior toward them. Brent calmly found someone to clean up the graffiti, and we continued on to the temple.

Brent and I paused briefly to put on the white shoe coverings that would help us keep the temple carpets clean. The shoe coverings were placed on our feet by a group of teenage volunteers, who were very pleased to perform this simple act of service.

As Brent and I entered the temple, we were joined by my niece Annie. We all walked together from one room to another. Brent pointed out the Syringa flower motif that had been created by a Utah artist and inlaid in most of the 200 glass window panes. The flowers etched on the glass were delicate and lovely.

My favorite pieces of art were the murals gracing the walls of the ordinance rooms, painted by an Idaho artist, who had faithfully captured many of the local landscapes. These scenes represented places in Idaho that I remembered and loved, most particularly the breath-taking majesty of Shoshone Falls. I could almost feel the heavy spray coming off the water. Shoshone Falls was a place I'd spent happy times as a child, enjoying picnics and marveling at the thundering water cascading down the rocks. In those days, we could walk down the steps to the bottom of the falls. Not anymore.

As we proceeded down the hall, we saw a group of volunteers coming toward us. Some of them were professional men and women with soft hands and designer clothes. Others were farmers dressed in simple but tasteful suits with gnarled hands and tanned faces. Together they came, side by side, across the floors of the temple. It was their pride in the temple that united them as they crossed its floors.

Their tithing monies had helped pay for its construction. They watched their temple grow and take shape in their community as they volunteered to tend its grounds, clean its walls, and crochet its altar cloths. But it was the joyful gleam in their eyes and the purpose in their strides that impressed me the most.

As Brent, Annie, and I moved to the elevator, we ran into Walt Petersen. Walt was also part of the temple committee. I shared a long and meaningful history with Walt. He'd been both bishop of our ward and our family doctor. Much more importantly than any of that, Walt had been instrumental in helping us adopt Alicia.

When we first began to suspect that we might not be able to get pregnant, I took comfort in knowing that my dad, who had done the legal work for several adoptions over the years, could help us if we decided to adopt. That was before my dad contracted pancreatic cancer.

One night, a few months after my dad was first diagnosed, my mother called us in a panic. My dad had unexpectedly slipped into a coma. Norm, Brent, and I jumped into our cars and immediately made the 3-hour drive from Salt Lake to Burley. (Dave was still on his mission in Palmyra, New York.) I prayed that my dad would still be alive when we arrived.

It seemed as though it took forever before my husband and I pulled up in front of Cassia Memorial Hospital. Before the keys were even out of the ignition, I bolted from the car and pushed impatiently through the sliding glass doors, walking quickly down the hall to my dad's room. "It's OK," my mom assured me, "he's just sleeping."

A few hours later my dad woke up and saw us all surrounding his hospital bed. "You're here because you thought I was dying," he choked tearfully. No one spoke.

"That's right, Dad," I eventually replied, as tenderly as I could, taking his hand in mine. My dad always expected honesty from his only daughter and eldest child. I could offer him nothing less now. But we all knew that the end was not far off.

The next morning, Doctor Walt asked to meet with us to talk to us about what we might expect during the final weeks of my dad's life. It wasn't an easy conversation. Death never is. But we all loved Walt Petersen. And we knew that he loved us. So we got through the conversation tearfully together.

As our meeting ended, I caught up with Walt as he was leaving. I told him we'd been having trouble getting pregnant. We'd been through endless doctor visits and tests. We were both contributing to the infertility, and it didn't look promising. "If we're still not pregnant in another 8 months or so, will you help us adopt, Walt?" I asked tears running down my face.

Walt put his arm around my shoulder, hugged me closely, and nodded. "Of course I will, Susan," he responded kindly.

I didn't tell my dad about my conversation with Walt that day. Walt never did either.

After spending a few more days with my dad, we told him good-bye again and drove back to Salt Lake. He seemed to be doing a little better. And we all had to get back to work.

The following Wednesday, I was sitting in my office at school correcting English papers for my class of juniors. An announcement came over the intercom: "Mrs. Swann to the office, please."

"Dad!" I said aloud, jumping up from my desk. I clattered down the stairs and made my way to the office.

"Phone call for you, Susan," someone said casually. I picked up the phone and pressed the flashing lighted button.

"Hello," I kind of croaked.

It was my dad on the phone. He sounded so happy, as he bellowed, "Susan! It's Dad!" Dad happy? He was dying.

"Guess what!?" he exclaimed. I couldn't imagine.

He rushed on. "A little baby girl was just born on her way to the hospital. Her mother has decided to put her up for adoption."

His words came even faster now. "Walt came in and asked me if I knew anyone who wanted to adopt a baby." His voice broke now. "I told him you wanted a baby, Susan."

Dear, sweet Walt. Bless you for not telling Dad that I talked with you last week. And thank you for putting us at the top of your long list of hopeful parents who were waiting for a baby.

Dad went on excitedly. "I'm here holding her now, Susan. She's beautiful! And she's yours if you want her." He paused to take a breath. I hadn't yet been able to say anything. "You do want her, don't you, Susan?"

"Of course I do, Dad!" I answered, my mind still racing over the idea that I'd just become a mother in the last 5 minutes. I hadn't even talked to my husband yet. I didn't have a crib. Or clothes. Or a room ready. I was still teaching school. Calm, down. I told myself. This will all work itself out. You're going to be a mom!

"Was it ok that I got to hold her first . . . before you did," my dad asked, concerned now.

"Who better than you, Dad," I said. "Nothing makes me happier than to know you're holding her."

He didn't say anything for a minute. And then he said softly, "It's a life for a life, Susan." And we both just sobbed.

Three days later, my husband and I drove back to Burley. This time to pick up our new baby daughter. I laughed and I cried. And sometimes I did both at the same time. My dad came home from the hospital for a few hours to spend time with us and our new baby. He was growing very weak.

My dad died several weeks later. Alicia was the only grandchild he would ever see or hold. The last act of his life was to do something for his daughter that could never be measured: As he left this life, he left a new, precious life behind for our family.

And now here was Doctor Walt, standing in front of me again in the Twin Falls temple, clasping me tightly in a happy embrace. I hadn't seen him in years. His first question to me naturally was, "How's Alicia?"

"She's living in St. George with Jenna, and doing very well," I responded. "She's working as a medical assistant for an oncologist."

I think it seemed fitting to both of us that Alicia was working with cancer patients at the time, helping to both save and prolong life. Her grandfather would have liked that too. I was so proud of her. Alicia had been through more than her fair share of problems and came triumphantly out the other side. I thought about Ernest Hemmingway's comment: "Life breaks all of us. And some of us are strong at the broken places." That was my Alicia: She was strong at the broken places.

I smiled back up at Walt. He didn't look at all as though he were a man in his seventies. He was strong, active, and vibrant. He and his wife were getting ready to serve another medical mission for the Church. This time, somewhere in Central America, I think. They alternated back and forth between their children and grandchildren and delivering medical care in foreign countries. I realized that they were wearing themselves young in service to others.

I couldn't help but compare Walt to other retirees I knew. These retirees were people who enjoyed a good game of golf, a lively round of tennis, brisk laps in the pool, or endless games of cards. They were great people. But they seemed to have retired not just from work but from life itself. They were relaxed. Comfortable. But from where I sat, they didn't have the sense of purpose I saw in the retired volunteers I met that day in the temple with Brent.

What was it that gave them that energy? What was it that guided their actions? Whatever it was, I knew that I didn't have it. And I didn't really know how to get it. Or if I did, I didn't think I could believe as they believed. I had given all that up so long ago.

# XVII

## My Littlest Angel

*K*aty and Tyler's little Lucy was nearing her second birthday. Contrary to the unabashed joy with which she approached almost every other event in her young life, Lucy was not happy about turning two. Not happy at all. In her mind, there was something about being two that took her out of the realm of being a baby and pushed her squarely into toddlerhood. It was too much change, coming too fast, for her to wrap her little one-year old mind around.

The adults in her life, including me, were trying not to be amused by Lucy's tearful and angry protests over her upcoming birthday—although I for one could appreciate her efforts to try and stop time. I didn't want to get any older either.

One day in early August, with Lucy's second birthday just around the corner, I came to take her to dinner. We were going out for sandwiches and then to the park that had a pond to feed our leftovers to the ducks. Feeding the ducks was one of Lucy's favorite things to do. So I expected to find her in a happy mood.

Instead, she was sorting madly through her closets, pulling out old clothes and shoes and flinging them on the floor. She was trying desperately to make the too-small clothes fit, to no avail. She was particularly unhappy about a pair of pink gel sandals I'd given her a few months earlier. As I looked at the shoes, it was plain to see that they were absolutely too small for her feet.

As Katy tried to reason with her, Lucy burst into tears, her curly blonde hair falling limply into her soft, round face. She finally threw herself prostrate on the floor in sheer frustration. No one would ever accuse

Lucy of not being in touch with her feelings. It was one of the things I liked best about her.

In point of fact, I had adored Lucy from the first moment she began to be Lucy. She was bright, opinionated, affectionate, and an unabashed people person. Even toys were no fun for her unless there was someone around to share them with.

From the time she could talk, which was very early for her age, Lucy called me Sue-sue. (I had to remind my brothers that only Lucy was allowed to use that moniker.) Sometimes Lucy even called me "My Sue-sue." Especially after Claire came along. Who could resist that? Certainly not me.

Lucy and I really bonded the night she came to spend the night at my house. It was the night her little sister Claire was born. As Lucy walked happily into my house through the garage, I stopped to pick up the small, aquamarine folding chair I had bought just for her to use when she came to visit. We set it up in front of the large screen television.

After a dinner of mac and cheese and applesauce, we popped some popcorn and settled in to watch "Elmo's World." Several times. We sang songs along with Elmo and ate fruit snacks. It was definitely a party. It was great fun for both of us.

When it was finally time for bed, I took Lucy into my room and put her in the play pen I had bought for Alex to use whenever he decided to get married and have babies. Lucy didn't want to be alone in the room, and she didn't particularly care for the play pen, even though it was a Winnie-the-Pooh play pen. Possibly because it was blue and not pink. More likely because she wasn't in her own bed. And I think Lucy sensed change in the wind when her mommy and daddy went to the hospital to get her new sister. I lay down on my bed with the play pen at the foot of the bed, so she wouldn't be alone, and turned out the light.

Predictably, I suppose, she still wasn't happy. She kept saying, "Sue-sue's bed. Sue-sue's bed." I finally gave in, pulled her up out of the play pen, making sure to collect her blanket, her binky, and baby Pooh. I laid her next to me on one of my big pillows. I told her that if she wanted to lie in my bed, she would have to go to sleep. Obediently, she closed her eyes tightly.

Fifteen minutes passed. Lucy's breathing became deeper and more regular. I decided it might be safe to move her back to the play pen, so I could go to sleep at some point. As I started to move, Lucy reached over and tickled my cheek, breaking into peals of laughter. Of course, I laughed too.

I tried again to get Lucy to go to sleep. But the tickle Sue-sue's face game had become too enticing. I finally gave up, got up, and turned on the light. She was smiling at me. Who could be mad at that face? We read stories until Lucy fell asleep, quite in spite of her best efforts to stay awake. I laid her gently back in the play pen, sat cross-legged on the floor beside her, and just watched her sleep for awhile. I knew I wouldn't have her here with me forever. Law school would end and Tyler would move his little family to Idaho, buy a house, and join the family law practice. I wanted to enjoy Lucy while I could. I had been so busy when my own children were small. Too busy to just stop and watch them sleep. What a waste, I thought.

And I was grateful that Lucy had brought a sense of wonder and joy to my life that I hadn't had since Alicia, Alex, and Jenna were babies. Whenever Lucy saw me, she came running to me, her little arms pumping, until she flung herself into my out-stretched arms, and promptly laid her head on my shoulder. Then we just paused to enjoy the moment. I so loved Lucy.

Lucy is also a firm believer in her Heavenly Father and in "the Jesus Christ," which is what she called him then. One day, as May wore into June, I was over at Katy's house for dinner. As we sat down to eat, Katy asked Lucy who should say the blessing on the food. I think we both expected Lucy to volunteer herself. She loved saying the prayer on the food. But to both Katy and my surprise, Lucy pointed her finger at me from her little high chair and said, "Sue-sue."

Katy and I both knew that I hadn't prayed in years. Katy couldn't remember ever hearing me pray. There was a very small, awkward silence as I considered Lucy's request. Since I would have done almost anything to keep from disappointing Lucy, I turned to her and said, "I'd be happy to say the blessing, Lucy. Thank you."

And so for the first time in a long time, I bowed my head and offered thanks for the food. When I finished my prayer, Lucy said "Aaaamen," and smiled at me approvingly.

That was the first time I had prayed with Lucy. But there would be many more times to come. As young as she was, praying was part of her life. When I tended her while Katy went to relief society meetings, right after she brushed her teeth, put on her pink and green princess pajamas, drank another glass of water, and helped me read the umpteenth story, Lucy and I knelt by her little bed and prayed together. She said the prayer. And I listened as Lucy talked to God. She blessed her mom and dad, her new baby sister, both sets of grandparents, her aunts and uncles . . . and her Sue-sue.

How could I be untouched by Lucy's humble and sincere prayers? When Lucy prayed to her Heavenly Father, she really prayed to her Heavenly Father. She was the epitome of child-like faith. I think I might have understood for the first time what Christ meant when he said, "Unless ye become as a little child." He was talking about Lucy. Lucy's world was full of wondrous questions and decisive answers. I admired her for that. And I couldn't help but be affected by her simple faith in God.

Sometimes Lucy and I also took walks together along the levee, waving at passing boaters or stopping to pet someone's dog. Lucy was so enchanting with her curly hair and infectious grin that people were more than happy to stop and let Lucy pet their animals. "She's darling!" was the usual comment. As her great-aunt, I just beamed and agreed. I might have said thank you. I'm not sure. I was sure that I was looking at the world newly minted through Lucy's eyes. And I decided that maybe it really was a wondrous place after all.

And now Lucy was finally ready to turn two. I couldn't believe it, I thought, as I walked into the bakery to pick up her cake. As I opened the door, I saw Lucy's pink princess cake with the big silver crown on top sitting on the counter. I just knew she was going to love it! The sales clerk gently placed Lucy's cake in the pink box and taped it closed. I paid her and hurried out the door. I was running a little late from work, and I knew that everyone would be anxiously awaiting the arrival of both me and the cake.

By the time I walked into the restaurant, Katy, Lucy, Tyler, and Claire were finishing the appetizers. "Sue-sue!" Lucy called across the room from her booster chair. I apologized for being late, and after hugs all around, I placed the box with the cake carefully on the table in front of Lucy.

Lucy's eyes grew wide as Katy pulled the cake from the box. "It has a crown," she whispered in awe. She clapped her little hands to her cheeks in surprise and then clapped them in front of her for joy. Katy removed the crown from her cake, wiped off the frosting, and placed the crown on Lucy's head. She smiled up at all of us and looked like the little princess that she was. "Thank you, Sue-sue!" she exclaimed loudly as her mom took a picture.

Lucy's tears over her transition to a big girl had vanished. She'd faced up to the first big challenge of her life and had come away victorious. And who would expect anything less from Lucy?

As for me, Lucy's exuberant love of life and her faith in God had changed me. Lucy was another important touch with the Spirit, as my heart continued to heal, and I moved one step closer to my own return to faith.

# XVIII

## Searching New Landscapes

*I* was getting ready to take my first real vacation in too long. In my mind, it was actually more of an adventure than a vacation. I'd been preserving time off and saving my pennies to go to Australia for what promised to be 26 glorious days. I was so eager to go! Fortunately my boss was supportive. "Take some time off. Get away. You've earned it," he told me. "We'll take care of things while you're gone."

I was traveling to Australia on my own, which is how I initially wanted it to be, until it came right down to the night I was leaving. As I sat waiting for my flight to board, I called my children. They were all together laughing and talking and enjoying a post-Christmas dinner without me. Alex put his cell phone on speaker and laid it on the table so they could all hear me. It was Alex's Karry who sensed the uneasiness in my voice.

"Are you a little nervous, Susan?" she asked gently.

"I think I am a little," I said. Truthfully I was more than a little nervous. But a little was all I was willing to admit to being at the moment.

"You're going to have a great time, Mom!" Alex said. "Don't worry."

"Have fun, Grandma!" Jenna offered.

"And don't forget to email us," Alicia added.

"I will," I said. "Guess I'd better get going. They're calling my flight. I love you guys!"

"We love you too!" They all said almost in unison. "Have a good time!" And then they were gone.

I reminded myself that I'd always wanted to go to Australia, ever since I was a child. Mostly because my dad made it sound like a magical place filled with kangaroos, didgeridoos, and kookaburras. He was in the army during World War II, stationed in the Pacific. He spent his leave in Australia, which he loved. The rest of the time, he was fighting in either New Guinea or the Philippines. Similar to most men of his generation, he didn't much care for talking about the war. He'd made it back alive. That seemed to be enough for him.

Occasionally he shared a rare glimpse into what his life had been like for him then. He talked about the daily bombing raids that came like clockwork in the middle of the night. They didn't do much actual damage, because they were so predictable. But they served to disrupt sleep, leaving the men tired the next day. "When we heard the air raid siren," he said, "we'd run for the fox holes. The fox holes were usually filled with water and rats. After we jumped in, we'd have to shake our pant legs to keep the rats from running up and down our legs. It didn't always work." That in and of itself sounded pretty terrible to me.

The only other thing I remember my dad telling me about the war was, "I was a trained killer then, Susan. You don't know that side of me." And he was right. I didn't. And the more I thought about it, the more I didn't want to. He was my hero dad who loved me unconditionally. I could do no wrong in his eyes. He encouraged me and kept me safe. That's the dad I wanted to know. I didn't want to know the trained killer he had buried so deeply inside himself when the war ended. So I contented myself with stories about Australia, which he loved to tell.

Dad told us about the Outback. He regaled us with tales of jumbucks and tucker bags, billabongs and swagmen waiting for their billy to boil. Sometimes he could even be found dancing around the house singing "Waltzing Matilda." I had no idea what it all meant, but it sounded exotic and wondrous to my young mind. My dad never said where he'd been in Australia or where it was he wanted to go back to. Or if he did, I was regrettably not paying attention. My dad died before he could ever get back to Australia. All we had left of his time there was an old boomerang and several Australian coins dated 1943.

So now I wanted to go to Australia. Partly to find a part of him and partly to find a part of me. I was looking for something. I didn't know what yet. But I expected to find answers in Australia. Soni cautioned me that I couldn't really plan an epiphany. While on some level I knew she was right, I was still going to look. So on the 27th day of December, 2008, I boarded my plane for Australia.

My first stop was Sydney. I was here for New Year's Eve, and I planned to spend it at the Opera House watching fireworks over the water. I was thrilled. Welcome to OZ! I said to myself. Before I left, I asked my brother Norm to be sure and watch the broadcast of the fireworks on television and think of me there, when he did.

He told me later, "I watched TV at midnight, and they replayed the fireworks at the Sydney Opera House. I was sure I saw a woman in a yellow dress standing at the window. I kept waiting for a caption on the screen to read "Susan Swann at the Sydney Opera House on New Year's Eve." The caption never came up, but I'm sure that was you!" Very funny, Norm. But it did turn out to be a magical night for me, nonetheless.

I wandered through the white cavernous clam-shell building that night and took my seat in the huge concert hall. The building acoustics proved to be truly incredible and more than lived up to their reputation. The program began with light, classical music and ended with Broadway show tunes. My dad would have loved the chilling rendition of "Old Man River." As a child, I remember lying in my bed at night, listening to my dad sing "Old Man River," and "In the Gloaming," as he spaded the ground outside my window. It made me feel safe and happy listening to him sing. Here's to you, Dad, I thought to myself, tears standing in my eyes. I wish we could have been here together tonight. You would have loved it.

The orchestra reached a crescendo at 11:00 p.m., as all 2,600 of us threw colored streamers, while tons of confetti was blown from little canons scattered around the hall. Thousands of balloons were released from the ceiling amid cries of "Happy New Year," and strains of "Auld Lang Sine." And then we walked outside to see the fireworks.

Moments later, the span of the Harbour Bridge exploded in light. It was unlike anything I'd ever seen before. The "Oohs" and "Aaahs" that broke out over the crowd didn't begin to do justice to the display. The theme was "Creation." That seemed fitting for the beginning of a new year, I thought. I had no idea at the time just how meaningful that theme would be as events that were yet to transpire in my life unfolded in early 2009.

It was in the Opera House on another day that I also became vicariously acquainted with Bennelong. As the story was told to me, Bennelong was an Aborigine who'd been in Australia when the English first landed. He was captured by the English in 1789, taken to England, and presented as a curiosity to King George. While Bennelong was in London, he learned English and took to serious drinking. After the English grew tired of him, and he was finally returned to Australia six years later, his hut had been torn down and his wife had left him for someone else. He quite naturally grew despondent.

Bennelong was now neither English nor Aborigine. He was caught between two cultures and didn't belong to either one. He'd been gone too long from his people, and he couldn't find a way back. Bennelong died all alone, broke, and an alcoholic in 1813. That sounded as though it were an awful end to anyone's life.

As I heard Bennelong's story, I thought about how difficult and lonely it can be for people to be on the outside of their cultures. I'd experienced no shortage of that myself. It was then that I began thinking about the possibility of dipping a toe back in my own. Could I regain my faith? I might not even enjoy being at church. I didn't think the way they did anymore. Maybe too much had transpired in the interim, I reasoned. But the question remained with me nonetheless.

My next stop was Cairns. The day we motored out to the reef, I signed up on board for an introductory scuba diving lesson. Seemed like a good idea at the time. After donning my stinger suit, which was meant to protect me from deadly jelly fish, I boarded a small skiff with 10 other divers and motored over to the beach to practice. Our crew had already provided us with some basic tips on how to equalize the pressure in our ears once we went under, and how to use our air regulators. It turned out I was the oldest one who had signed up for the dive. The youngest one in our group was a mere boy of 17, so the two of us got our own guide, Lani. After a brief lesson in the rolling water, Lani asked us if we still wanted to make the dive. I wasn't so sure anymore. But the kid said yes. What else could I do?

Lani pulled the cord that let the air out of my life jacket, and my weight belt started to pull me under. I felt more than a little panicky. I quickly flashed the signal to go back up, which we did. At that point, I was ready to back out. As we broke the surface, Lani calmly reminded me that I was a good swimmer, and that I'd be fine. "Are you really sure I can do this?" I asked her, struggling to maintain my balance as another wave swept over me, knocking me off my feet. The kid just treaded water, hoping I'd make up my mind soon.

Lani said, "If you think you can, you can." Shades of my dad.

My dad told me over and over, "You can be anything you want to be, princess. Do anything you want to do. Remember that." Ok, Dad, I thought. So with some misgivings, I rather weakly said, "Let's go."

We began again slowly sinking into the water, swimming down about 25 feet. Visions of the old television series "Sea Hunt" that I used to love watching with my dad flashed through my mind, as I conjured up images of terrifying bends and painful decompression chambers. Where are you when I need you, Lloyd Bridges? Then I reminded myself that we were only down 25 feet and pushed on.

I concentrated on breathing in and out slowly and deeply through the regulator and tried to stay focused on the brightly colored fish, coral, and giant clams that surrounded me. I saw white and orange clown fish, beaked coral fish, little yellow fish in schools, and a small manta ray. But it was the coral that was so unusual, varied, and positively breathtaking.

I had rented an underwater camera for the day, so when that little feeling of panic started coursing through my veins again, I focused on taking pictures and reminded myself to breathe and look around. What I saw was a whole new world.

We were down a total of about 30 minutes. Eventually Lani signaled that we were going up, and we made our way up slowly, surfacing behind the boat. (The boat was there, so that was good. We hadn't been left behind on the Great Barrier Reef.) I was pretty happy to shuck my life jacket and strip off the weight belt. I was relieved to be back on board.

But I'd done it! I made the dive. I heard later that more than a few Japanese tourists faint out there in the ocean and some Americans panic and have heart attacks. I did no such thing. So I stood a little taller that day.

The next day my group boarded a train in Cairns to go up through the mountains to Kuranda. After wandering in and out of the shops for awhile, we caught a bus up to the Daintree Rainforest station, where we found, much to my delight, a 1942 amphibious army Duck waiting to take us through the rainforest. Not many of those left in the world! I could picture my dad riding one of these Ducks through the jungle when he was in the war. I loved the whole idea of it.

We traveled across rutted roads and then drove right through a lake. I looked around at plants that were millions of years old. We saw a large nest filled with thousands of huge, white termites in front of us swarming and drilling their way down through a tree. Our driver also pointed out a bearded dragon, and a saw-back turtle. Not your typical day in the park. I hated exiting the Duck at the end of the ride, but lunch on the barbie was calling our names.

After lunch, we went up to an amphitheatre to watch Aboriginal dancing. One of the dancers took us on a "dreamtime" walk, back to the traditions of his ancestors. I had read in Wikipedia that "the dreaming" is a sacred era in which ancestral Totemic Spirit Beings formed The Creation. In "The Last Wave," a 1977 Australian film directed by Peter Weir, the statement is made:

"Aboriginals believe in two forms of time; two parallel streams of activity. One is the daily objective activity, the other is an infinite spiritual cycle called the 'dreamtime,' more real than reality itself. Whatever happens in the dreamtime establishes the values, symbols, and laws of Aboriginal society. It was believed that some people of unusual spiritual powers had contact with the dreamtime."

Aborigines also believed that people's souls existed before they became physical. This eternal part of them is said to exist before an individual is born and continues after she dies. I was enchanted by the Dreamtime and recognized parallels to my own Mormon heritage. I had once believed in a pre-existence. I had once believed in life eternal. I just didn't anymore. But did that mean I never would again? I didn't know.

The next morning at 4:00 a.m., we bid goodbye to Cairns and

boarded a flight for Melbourne. After checking into the hotel, I went to Queen Victoria Market via tram. On the tram, I met a 20-something woman, who was also traveling on her own. She was from Canada and was a free lance animator for various websites. She had decided that she could live anywhere in the world to do the kind of work she did, so she applied for a one-year work visa to live in New Zealand. She didn't know yet where she was going to live, but after she finished touring Australia, she told me she planned to interview cities and find a place to live in New Zealand. That sounded wonderfully adventurous to me. Much more adventurous than my 26 day trip through Australia. Suddenly I didn't feel so alone.

"Will you be going to New Zealand as well?" she asked me.

"I wish I could," I answered her. "But my time's limited and I still have lots of Australia left to see. Maybe another time." As I said that, I doubted I'd ever be back in this part of the world again. But one year later I was in New Zealand visiting Brent and Marcia, who by then would be living not in Twin Falls, but in Auckland. You just never know.

I alighted at Queen Victoria Market, wished my young friend well, and started making my way through dozens and dozens out of at least 1,000 stalls. As I walked around the market, I found the perfect didgeridoo or "dige" for Alex. It was beautifully painted by a local Aboriginal artist. I bought the didgeridoo along with a cover that had a sling for my shoulder and left happy. Never mind that I would have to drag this didgeridoo with me across half of Australia.

I loaded my new purchase onto the tram and unintentionally took the long way back to the Radisson. I had tickets that night to see the musical *Wicked*. I'd wanted to see this play for months! The concierge who sold me the tickets in Sydney assured me that it was better than the London production.

As I sat down to watch the play, I found the sets stunning, the costumes gorgeous, the lighting glitzy, and the voices powerful. I hadn't heard much about the plot before going, although I knew that it was the story of the Wizard of Oz told from the witch's point of view, rather than Dorothy's. I'd always loved looking at events from multiple points of view. This was going to be fun!

The theme of the play revolved around prejudice, small mindedness, and the empty seduction of fame. My favorite song in the play was "Wonderful," sung by the wizard himself. My favorite lines from that song went something like "We believe lots of things that aren't true. We call them history." Those words elicited a laugh from everyone in the audience, including me. While it was funny, it was also true. So much history depends on whose perspective of events is accepted.

The wizard seemed to agree with me, as he hopped and jigged his way around the stage singing, "A man's called a traitor or liberator . . . It's all in which label continues to persist." I wondered about the conflicting viewpoints on my own religious history. Where did the truth lie? Had I accepted the right version of events since I'd left the Church? I still didn't know. All I knew at that moment was that it was another magical evening in Oz.

The next day, we drove to the Serendip Open Range Sanctuary, where we were immediately among kangaroos, emus, and cockatoos. We found a few mobs of kangaroos, including some joeys with their mums. We then stopped by a small billabong filled with birds, attracted by the water. (So that's what a billabong is, Dad!) When we finally broke for our picnic lunch, Paul made us billy tea accompanied by Anzac biscuits.

Paul cooked our tea in a tin pot filled with lemon leaves and then swung the "bill" around in a circle, utilizing centrifugal force to keep the tea in the pot while it mixed with the leaves. I'd never seen anything like it. So here I was, a waltzing Matilda out in the bush with the kangaroos, waiting for the billy to boil. (Imagine that, Dad!)

I found that I was falling in love with Australia and its people, just as my dad had. The Australians I'd met all seemed to expect a certain amount of trouble out of life. And when it came, they took it in stride, similar to the day the "air con" went out on the train. No big deal. No complaints. Could I learn something from the Australians by expecting, rather than being surprised by, problems along the way?

The next day it was time to move on again. By now I'd seen the Reef and the Opera House and points in between. But I had yet to see the Rock. After spending a few days in Adelaide, I flew to Alice Springs. The next morning Emu tours picked me up from my hotel, and we began our very long trek on the very straight track out to Ayer's Rock, or Uluru, as the Aborigines call it.

As we drove sleepily along the red sands of the semi-arid desert, our guides Tony and Des traded off driving and sleeping, which was a good plan, given both the length of the trip and the monotony of the straight road. They served us a light breakfast of cheese, crackers, juice, and fruit twists as we rode. Both Tony and Des were knowledgeable and friendly. Their commentary was laced with an abundance of the uniquely Aussie sense of humor, which seemed to be magnified in the vast stretches of the Outback.

With the occasional pit stop, it took us about 5 hours to reach Uluru from Alice Springs. As we neared Uluru, we stopped first at the Olgas for a short hike. It was here that it became clear to me why fly netting was such an essential piece of gear out here. After dragging my fly hat with me all over the continent, I really put it to good use today. There were too many flies to make swatting them an effective alternative to netting, I thought, as six huge black flies sat resting comfortably on the netting covering my face.

But it was the Rock I had come to see. And at last, there it was: This huge sandstone monolith rising up from the desert floor literally out of nowhere. It was truly magnificent. And it wasn't difficult to see why Uluru is sacred to the Aborigines. It was an awe-inspiring place that was difficult to describe in any way that did it justice.

I found that the Rock itself changes color throughout the day, depending on how the sun strikes its face. The closer I got to the rock, the more varied it became, pocked with water holes, rock art, and caves. It was an impressive, imposing, and silent place that demanded a certain reverence.

After exploring a small part of the Rock's base, we eventually drove over to a large, open area for a barbecue and a sunset viewing of Uluru. Tony and Des had stowed stoves and food under the bus. They soon had a delicious meal of snags (sausages) and onion cooking on the barbie. Combined with 6 different kinds of salads, we enjoyed every bite. The food tasted good in the cooling desert air. The flies had called it a day, so eating our meal was a pleasant experience as we watched the sun set through pink clouds over Uluru.

I kept snapping pictures, hoping to capture the ever changing color of the rock. I thought about how carefree I'd felt the past several weeks just having the time to take pictures. Armed with my camera, I watched for just the right subject to shoot and waited for just the right light and the right angle to get just the right the picture. Looking at the world through the lens of my camera shifted my own focus in ways that I found therapeutic.

None of us was in a hurry that evening, so we just sat around talking in the shadow of this 350 million year old rock. We spoke about Uluru and Australia and how much we loved seeing new places and thinking new thoughts. I could feel the door to my mind swinging open out there in the vast desert. What would later fill its empty spaces, I did not know at the time.

A few days later, my adventure ended and it was time to go home. I'd escaped for a time to what for me was sunny, "no worries" Australia. No cell phone. No Blackberry. No constant connection. Every day in Australia brought something new to wonder about or someone new to meet. What a sweet escape! One that I'd never forget and never regret making. It had been a grand adventure for me.

After I got home, I wondered if I'd found the answers I was looking for. I didn't think I had yet. But I'd raised some important questions. My epiphany was yet to come. What I still didn't understand was something Marcel Proust knew: "The real voyage of discovery consists not in searching new landscapes, but in having new eyes."

# XIX

# A Kind and Gentle Heart

*I*t was March of 2009 and just a few weeks since I'd gotten back from Australia. It was late one night when Alex called me. "Hi, Mom," he said.

"Hi son," I replied, a little sleepily. He didn't typically call this late.

"How are you, Mom?" he asked.

"I'm fine, son. Are you ok?"

"I'm in the emergency room," he answered steadily.

"You're where?!" I shouted over the phone, now fully awake. "Why?!"

"It's my appendix. The doctor thinks it might have to come out . . . tonight."

My first thought was that Alex was alone. I have a hard and fast rule about anyone being in a hospital alone and sick. It was now late enough that I couldn't get a flight out until morning. Who would be there with him for his surgery?

"Are you there by yourself, Alex?" I asked concerned.

"Yes. But Karry's on the way."

Karry! Of course. Karry would be there with him, I thought, relieved. "Please have her call me when she gets there," I told him.

"Ok, Mom. I will. Don't worry."

When Karry got to the hospital, she called me. "I can't get there until morning, Karry," I said concerned.

"Don't worry," she assured me. "I'll take care of everything." And she did. She called me every hour or so and gave me detailed reports on the unfolding situation. She asked the doctors the same questions I would have asked, if I'd been there. Karry was there when they wheeled Alex into surgery. And she sat up waiting for him all night.

I called her again on my way to the airport the next morning. "How's he doing?" I asked anxiously.

"They just took him into recovery," she said. "The doctors got it all out. His appendix was big enough to rupture, but it didn't. They got it in time. So don't worry. He's doing just fine." I cried tears of relief most of the way to the airport.

When I finally got to Alex's hospital room, he was sitting up in bed, a bit groggy, but looking none the worse for wear. Karry was still curled up sleepily in the chair next to him. I hugged her tightly and thanked her. "Now that you're here, Susan, I'm going to go home and take a shower," she said. When she saw the look on Alex's face, she promised she'd be back soon and kissed him goodbye.

Alex was asleep again within minutes. As I sat by his bedside watching him sleep, I smiled thinking about when Alex and Karry had first met. Alex was working retail a few nights a week to earn extra money. By day, he was an inside sales rep for a large company. By night, he sold men's suits. At least that's what he was hired to do. That's what he told *me* he was doing.

While he apparently did sell his fair share of suits, whenever he got the chance, he would wander the store and chat with saleswomen in the make-up, perfume, and accessories departments. He was such a friendly guy to everyone he met. The other employees quickly dubbed him "the mayor."

Alex was particularly attracted to the manager of the accessories department. Her name was Karry. There was no doubt that he was interested in her. The problem for Alex was that she wasn't all that interested in him. Rejection wasn't a typical part of Alex's dating experiences—until he met Karry.

Karry was an attractive, confident, and smart career woman who, at the time, was between relationships. When Alex asked her out, she politely refused. What did she want with someone who was nicknamed the mayor? How serious could he be about anything?

Alex tried to invite her out to eat and was rebuffed yet again. This time he left his business card on the top of the glass counter where Karry was standing. He had penned in his cell phone number. At least she could see that he had a serious job by day, even if he was the mayor by night. Karry thought he was pretty bold leaving his card after she'd told him no twice. But she kept it and tucked it into the far corner of her purse.

A few weeks later, on a whim, Karry decided to call Alex. Maybe it was his wide, pearly white grin. Maybe it was his big, brown, puppy-dog eyes. Or maybe it was because he was almost a foot taller than she was. Who knows what possessed her to make the call? But she did. And the rest, as they say, is history. And that was how Alex met Karry.

The day I first met Karry was over Easter brunch at Splashes restaurant in Laguna Beach. Alex and I'd been here several times, and we loved the stunning ocean-close views out the windows. The food is good, and there's almost always a fire burning in the grate to ward off the slight chill of the ocean air. So when Alex asked me to take him and Karry somewhere special for brunch, I suggested Splashes.

I knew that if Alex wanted me to meet Karry, she must be an important someone in his life. I always wanted to meet the girls Alex dated, but there weren't that many he wanted to bring home to meet his mom. As I sat across the table from Karry, I found her to be smart, focused, and politely reserved. She was obviously a serious contender for my son's affections. I'm guessing that I was scrutinizing her pretty carefully over my salmon hash and crème brûlée.

The next time I met Karry was when Alex brought her to Snowbird for our family's summer week at Iron Blossom Lodge. Not only did Alex want Karry to meet his mom, he wanted her to meet his sister, his niece, and our entire extended family. He wasn't just bringing someone to dinner this time: He was bringing someone to be part of the family.

The next day, Dave took us all out on his boat to go water skiing and wake boarding. When it was my turn, I went with Alex and Karry. Karry had never wake boarded before. After watching how much fun my nephew Matt was having, she was determined to give it a try.

"Are you sure you wouldn't rather water ski?" I asked her? That would have been my choice. I'd never been up on a wake board.

"Leave her alone, Mom," Alex said. "She knows what she's doing." He helped Karry put the wake board in the water. Karry slid into the water behind the boat and grabbed on to the board. Alex threw her the rope, and Dave inched the boat forward slowly, paying out the line. When Karry was ready, she called, "Hit it," and Dave jammed the throttle forward.

She was up! At least for the moment. A few seconds later, she bounced off, the wake board flying in the air behind her. But she had made it up on the first try. The next time, she stayed on. She gave the thumbs up sign to go faster. She looked as though she was having fun— At least until Dave took one of the turns too sharply. Then she face planted. Hard. She came up gasping for air. Dave circled around to pick her up, and Alex pulled both her and the wake board back into the boat. Dave was impressed that Karry was such a natural athlete. In that respect, she was similar to Alex.

A few days later, Alex and Karry and I were traveling down the canyon to Salt Lake for the 4th of July fireworks. I was surprised when Karry told me that Alex wanted to raise his children in the Mormon Church. Not only had the two of them been talking about marriage, but Alex was apparently thinking about going back to the Church. The conversation took my breath away. I'm not sure what I said, but I'm quite certain it was something both inane and obvious, such as, "It sounds as though the two of you have been talking about getting married and having a family."

"We're just talking, Mom," Alex said.

When we finally got to Holladay Park, the rest of the family was already waiting for us. I was feeling a bit shaken. I left Alex and Karry and went and sat down on a blanket by my niece Emily and her little son, Justin. I tousled his red hair and gave him a relieved hug.

Meanwhile, Karry stood over by Brent and Marcia, asking them questions about the Church. I guessed she needed to know what she was getting in to, if she were expected to raise her as yet unborn children in the Church.

Brent was very taken with Karry's interest in the Church. As were Dave and Norm. I, on the other hand, was neutral to confused. What did it all mean? What did I really know about Karry? What did I know about her heart and how she might treat my son, and now, it sounded as though, my grandchildren—who would also apparently be going to Primary.

*All* of my family said Karry seemed as though she were a really good person: Alicia, my 3 brothers and their wives, my mom, and all my nieces and nephews. And most especially Jenna. Jenna just adored her. I knew that Karry was beautiful, smart, mature, an amazing cook, and an incredible athlete. But what did I know about how she would love and care for my son? What did I know about her heart?

That question was answered for me today, I thought, as I heard Alex snoring softly after his surgery. Karry has a kind and gentle heart. And I knew Alex would be safe with her. It was an important turning point in my relationship with Karry.

But the day Karry and I bonded forever was one day when we were again at Snowbird. It was after I had come back to the Church, and Alex and Karry had been married for several months. I'd stubbed my big toe on the bed and ripped the nail. After hopping around in pain, I sat down to look at the nail. It was not a pretty sight. I didn't want to cut it, because I was pretty sure that was going to make it hurt even worse. When Karry surveyed the damage, she advised me to cut it off right away. She told me it would catch on something. Of course she was right.

She asked me if I'd brought toe nail clippers with me. Regrettably, but not surprisingly, I hadn't. I rarely come prepared for events that require tools of any kind. Karry, on the other hand, is always prepared for any eventuality. So she ran upstairs to find her clippers. When she brought them back downstairs, I reached out my hand to take them from her.

Instead of giving them to me, she knelt in front of me on the floor and began cutting my toe nail. I said, "Are you actually going to cut my toe nail for me?"

"Why wouldn't I?" she asked, as if it were the most natural thing in the world to cut your mother-in-law's toenail. I was pretty sure I never would have cut my mother-in-law's toenail.

Even Alex said, "I'm not sure I would cut your toenail, Mom. And I'm your son."

"I know what you mean, Alex," I replied.

Karry went straight to work on the nail and got it nicely clipped and trimmed. She was tender and gentle. It didn't even hurt. I was so grateful. "This is the same as Naomi and Ruth," I observed, touched by Karry's kindness.

"Who's that?" Karry wondered.

"There's a wonderful story in the bible about a mother-in-law and her loyal daughter-in-law, whose name is Ruth. We'll have to read it together sometime."

Later, when I told Soni about what Karry had done for me, she immediately responded, with no provocation from me, "The same as Naomi and Ruth!"

"Thank you!" I told her. "That's just exactly what I said."

Then I told Susan how Karry had cut my toe nail. Without hesitation, she responded, "The same as Naomi and Ruth!"

"Thank you!" I told her. "That's just exactly what I said." I love my friends. They get it. And I had found that not only was Karry good to my son, she was good to me too.

And Ruth said, "Intreat me not to leave thee, or to return from following after thee: for whither thou goest, I will go; and where thou lodgest, I will lodge: thy people shall be my people, and thy God, my God." (Ruth 1: 16)

# PART 4

# A HEART TRANSFORMED

*Be ye transformed by the renewing of your minds.*

—ROMANS 12:2

# XX

# A Return to Faith

The first Saturday in April began the same as many Saturday mornings do, which is to say that it wasn't especially unusual. Alex was mending nicely from his surgery, and my trip to Australia was fading into a distant memory, I thought reluctantly, as I slid out from under my warm covers and got out of bed. I pulled on my sweats and went outside to retrieve the morning paper.

After checking the headlines, I showered and ate breakfast. What to do next? I was having lunch with a friend, but that wasn't until later. I thought about calling Katy to see what she and the girls were up to, and then I remembered she and Tyler had driven to Utah for General Conference. My extended family would all be watching conference from somewhere, just as they always did: either in person, or on TV.

Casting about for something to do for a few hours, and not wanting to clean the house, I made the atypical decision to turn on General Conference and see what the Church might be telling the saints today. I curled up on the sofa and clicked on the TV. The choir was just singing the opening song. I always loved listening to the choir, so it was a good time to tune in.

I listened to speaker after speaker. I found that I wasn't disturbed by anything anyone said. That was highly unusual for me. In fact, I even agreed with most of what was said. Surprisingly, I ended up watching conference for the entire two hours, rather than switching it off either early or mid-way through the session. That's really strange, I thought. What's changed? But I had no more time to think about it. I was going to be late for lunch if I didn't leave immediately.

We eventually settled on Mexican food for lunch. Somewhere just before the check arrived, the phone on my Blackberry rang. I neither answered it nor looked to see who was calling. After lunch, we walked across the plaza to see a movie. As the lights dimmed, and before I shut down my phone, I checked to see who'd called me earlier. Maybe it was one of my children. I looked at the display. It wasn't Alicia or Alex. It was Brent. I wondered why he'd call me at this point in the day. Wasn't he in conference?

As I looked at his name on my screen, the words came clearly to my mind: Brent's calling to ask you to watch the afternoon session of conference. Was that true? I checked the message on my phone. That's what it said. I was more than a little surprised. In the middle of all this, the movie started. I so wished I could leave and just go home! Instead I fidgeted my way through the rest of the movie, wishing I were home instead of sitting in some random movie that I was barely paying attention to.

After the film ended, I made the short drive home, wondering again about what had happened earlier. While I was still on the road, a much stronger impression came to my mind, plainly with the words: "Your family needs you." I was stunned. And then the words: "It's time to go back to the Church." I was shocked and confused. But the messages that came to my agnostic mind were clear. I couldn't deny what I had experienced. Although there were several days that followed when I wished I could.

I talked with Brent later that evening. After listening to the events of his day, I described the events of mine. Brent was almost as amazed as I was. Almost, but not quite. Earlier that morning, after the opening song, Marcia showed him a note she'd written in her journal. It read: "It's time to invite Susan back to the Church." He'd nodded in agreement. My head was spinning as I heard Brent's words. I still didn't know what to make of it all.

The next day was Sunday. And I supposed that I'd better be thinking about finding a way to go back to church. So I tuned into conference. President Uchtdorf was speaking about "The Way of the Disciple." He said that discipleship was a journey that wasn't meant to be a spectator sport. He said it was "time to get off the sidelines." His statement took me back. I found myself asking, 'What are you doing on the sidelines?

That doesn't seem like you. Now instead of wondering why I was coming back to the Church, I was wondering why I'd ever left at all. It was a seismic and sudden shift in my thinking.

President Uchtdorf went on to advise that the first step on the path back begins in the exact place where we're standing. I was relieved to hear that. Could I really begin my journey back from the exact place on which I stood? Then President Uchtdorf promised that we could learn from our mistakes and be made whole.

I hadn't believed in God for so many years. What to do next? Maybe I could slowly build my belief back in both God and the Church, one brick at a time, through reading and study, until my house of faith was rebuilt. That was the only sensible plan I could come up with at the moment.

The next Sunday I went to church at the Scholar Way building. That was at least a place to start, I hoped. I seemed to be ok, as I sat through sacrament meeting. After the meeting ended, I saw Bishop Sopp coming down from the stand and heading in my direction. To my mind came the words, "Go talk with the Bishop." What I told myself in response was, maybe next week. Let's not get ahead of ourselves here. And I exited the pew. But people were in the aisle blocking my way, and I couldn't get by them.

Before I knew it, Bishop Sopp was at my side. He said hello and shook my hand. He'd met me once before, when he'd come caroling at my house this past Christmas with the Primary children. I said hello back and then blurted out, "I think I'm coming back to the Church." That was a pretty abrupt beginning, I thought. But I didn't know how else to say it. Bishop Sopp wasted no time in walking me right over to his executive secretary to set up an appointment for the coming Wednesday night.

As Wednesday drew closer, I almost called and canceled. Then I decided against it. I should probably meet with the bishop. See what he had to say. Maybe more importantly, see what I had to say. Whatever that might be. I wasn't feeling particularly in charge of my own destiny at the moment. It felt as though I was being led along, and I wasn't used to that.

Wednesday night, I pulled into the Church parking lot and walked around the building until I found an open door. I wasn't even certain where the Bishop's office was. I finally found it, took my seat outside on a folding metal chair, and waited my turn. I felt very uncomfortable sitting there.

Bishop Sopp came out and invited me in. We chatted a bit. I found out that he was an attorney, just like my dad and Brent. That made me feel comfortable in some strange way. He was very kind and very patient. He was relaxed. And he had a good sense of humor.

Then he asked me where I was in terms of the Church. "Think mustard seed," I said. He smiled and seemed to know exactly what I meant. He started talking about another inactive woman in our ward who had just come back to the Church. I told him about what had happened to me at conference. He didn't seem all that surprised.

Then he started talking about the atonement, and what miracles he'd seen it create in so many lives. I hadn't even gotten to that step yet in my mind. Things were moving a little fast for me. But as I left, we decided to meet again. In the meantime, I agreed to keep coming to church. At least I knew how to do that much.

But where to go from here? I had absolutely no idea. How should I begin reconstructing my faith? How could I make my little mustard seed sprout? I was rummaging through my bookshelf one day and found a book that I'd bought a few years ago and never read. It was written by Rabbi Harold Kushner. The title was, "Who Needs God?" Kushner's book seemed as if it might be a rational place to begin.

I also went online and ordered Henry Eyring's small book, "The Faith of a Scientist." I knew that Dr. Eyring had been a theoretical chemist by profession. He was a very smart man, who'd written about the compatibility of science and religion. He was also a man of great faith. He might be able to help me pull it all together.

Kushner's book took both a warm and practical approach to the subject of believing in God. He talked about why believing in God could be helpful. He discussed why the sacred was a desirable thing to have in anyone's life. He talked about the importance of religious communities. I found that I could accept most of what he said.

When Dr. Eyring's small book arrived in the mail a few days later, I read it more than once. The juxtaposition of science and religion, as he explained it, made sense to me. I reminded myself that people who were much smarter than I was had faith in God and believed the Book of Mormon to be the word of God. I picked up the Book of Mormon and again read the introduction, Joseph Smith's testimony, and the testimony of both the 3 witnesses and the 8 witnesses. It was a fantastic story. It was so fantastic, that it might just be true.

A few weeks passed. I continued attending church. Things started coming back to me much faster than I'd imagined. It had taken me a long time to leave the Church, so I thought coming back would take a long time too. But coming back was a very different proposition than leaving. I called my friend Susan and told her what was happening. She suggested that I start keeping a journal, which turned out to be a huge help to me.

About a month later, I arrived a bit late to church. I'd even thought about staying home. Maybe just do some studying on my own. But I'd promised myself and the bishop that I'd come every week. And a promise is a promise. So at the last minute, I urged myself to just get in the car and drive to church. Since I arrived a few minutes late, I sat on one of the back benches. I wasn't feeling particularly in tune, or in touch. But at least I was there.

Both talks given in the meeting that day were taken from Alma Chapter 5 and described the mighty change of heart. I quickly found myself overwhelmed by the words of both speakers. I was hanging on absolutely every word they said. I took out my scriptures and followed along. Alma's words seemed to leap off the page, and tears of joy began streaming down my cheeks. I understood for the first time what it meant to have my heart changed.

It was something real. And it wasn't an intellectual experience at all. It was a spiritual one. And it wasn't a slow change, as I had expected it to be. It was a literal transformation. At that moment, my little mustard seed of faith began sprouting all over the place, pushing itself through the soil of my heart. My life was being turned inside out in ways that were both sudden and jarring. I wouldn't have believed it, if I hadn't experienced it myself. My experience seemed incredible, even to me. But that didn't make it any less wondrous.

"The most beautiful experience we can have is the mysterious . . . Whoever does not know it and can no longer wonder, no longer marvel, is as good as dead, and his eyes are dimmed." Albert Einstein.

# XXI

# And I Came to Myself

*A* sense of the miraculous had returned to my life. It was as if I'd awakened from a deep sleep. I felt similar to the fictional Rip Van Winkle. It seemed as though I had been spiritually "asleep," as it were, for the past 14 years. And then one day, I suddenly woke up. I had no words that seemed adequate to describe the transformation that had taken place inside me.

I did know that the world around me looked fresh and new. It seemed as though a veil had been lifted from my eyes. Trivial objects and events that were once important to me became inconsequential. I had never experienced anything like it.

Bishop Sopp suggested that I read the story of the prodigal son in Luke 15. As I did, I found that the basic story was still recognizable to me: The prodigal son leaves his home and wastes his fortune. Then one day, he realizes he's "filling his belly with the husks that the swine eat."

His next words resonated with me in a way they never had before. The words were: "And he came to himself." I read them over and over: "And he came to himself." I think he meant it literally. To me, those words implied reframing his thinking in a sudden and startling new way. Similar to, "What was I thinking? How did I wake up and find myself in this place?"

I eventually searched the scriptures for references that related to awakening and change. I found that the whole awakening idea, having a change of heart, and experiencing transformation was outlined in many places in most of the standard works. Isaiah 52: 1, "Awake, awake. Put on thy strength." Ezekiel 11: 19, "And I will put a new spirit within you." Ephesians 5: 14, "Awake thou that sleepest, and arise from the dead and Christ shall give thee light." Alma 5:7, "Behold, he changed their hearts; yea he awakened them out of a deep sleep, and they awoke unto God." And my favorite, Romans 12:2, "Be ye transformed by the renewing of your minds."

It was becoming clear to me. I think almost every new convert to the Church, as well as those who have returned to activity after long absences, knows exactly what I'm talking about. My experience was not unique. It was just unusual for me.

As the story of the prodigal son continues, he too realizes that his life must change. He is filled with a desire to repent. He confesses to his father: "I have sinned . . . And I am unworthy." As I read those words, I knew that I also needed to make things right. I'd broken promises and covenants.

That's not to say that I was looking forward to the repentance process. I most certainly was not. I was convinced, however, that in order to begin again, I would have to take the Church's outlined and requisite steps to get me where I now knew I wanted to be.

I met with Bishop Sopp again. We talked for a long time. He spoke to me of repentance and Godly sorrow. I made a clean breast of my past mistakes. I felt unburdened. He listened with love and patience. He told me the Lord wanted me back.

He went on to remind me that while forgiveness was always possible and open to anyone, forgiveness did not erase consequences. I understood what he meant. I had two inactive children who were where they were because of me—which isn't to say that my activity would have guaranteed theirs. But my inactivity almost assured theirs as well. Bishop Sopp encouraged me to read the words of Enos. We would meet again in a few weeks.

I remembered nothing of Enos. So I went back and read his words again. The introduction to Enos Chapter 1 read: "Enos prays mightily and gains a remission of his sins." The operative word here seemed to be "mightily."

Then Enos 1:2, "And I will tell you of the wrestle which I had before God, before I received a remission of my sins." Enos 1:4, " . . . and all the day long did I cry unto him; yea, and when the night came, I did still raise my voice high that it reached the heavens."

That was nothing if not proscriptive. So, similar to Enos, I spent a full day fasting and praying. As I did so, I felt impressed to read what the scriptures said about forgiveness. I turned to Matthew 6: 14–15. I found, not surprisingly, that in order to be forgiven, I first had to forgive others.

But hadn't I done that already? As I thought back to an entry in my journal of just a few weeks ago, I recalled that it still contained residual anger over the divorce and the losses I had suffered so long ago. Guess I still hadn't fully forgiven others.

So today I was absolutely determined to do just that. I wanted to really *let go* this time. My return to the Church and my community of faith marked the restoration of so much that I'd lost. I didn't want to waste another minute looking back. So I took all the bitterness, sadness, emptiness, and regret and just flushed them from my soul.

I felt so free! And I continued to pray that I too might be forgiven. I prayed that I could return to my faith with a full purpose of heart.

When Enos prayed, he was told, "Enos, thy sins are forgiven thee, and thou shalt be blessed." When I finished my prayers, as night approached, to my mind came the words, "Because you have forgiven others, I also forgive you. Go your way, and sin no more."

"And I Enos knew that God could not lie; wherefore my guilt was swept away." (Enos 1:6)

My own sobs of relief over the loss of my guilt were covered over by sounds of pelting rain outside my bedroom window. While I knew the Church would still have to forgive me, I was certain that God already had.

"And I [Enos] said: "Lord, how is it done? And he said unto me: Because of thy faith in Christ, whom thou hast never before heard nor seen . . . wherefore, go to, thy faith hath made thee whole." (Enos 1:7–8)

It's impossible to adequately explain how I felt at that moment as I drifted off to sleep, to describe the joy and peace that flooded my heart. I was filled with the "peace that surpasseth understanding." I slept more soundly and more deeply that night than I had in 14 years.

I met again with the bishop the following week. I told him about my experience with repentance. I felt impressed to ask him for a blessing. In his blessing, he told me that my family's love and faith had brought me back to the Church.

Bishop Sopp then blessed me with the power of discernment. He told me to use my talents in the service of others. He counseled me to remember that there were many people who loved me. Then he blessed me that I would be able to return to the temple. There was nothing I wanted more than that.

After he finished his blessing, Bishop Sopp told me that he was still thinking about whether or not I had done all that I needed to do to move forward. I respected the fact that he took his job as a judge in Israel very seriously. He was helping me heal spiritually. These things take time. I told him I trusted him and would abide by any decision he made on my behalf. Those were new things for me to do.

Bishop Sopp thought and prayed about me for 3 more weeks. I tried to sit patiently in church on Sundays, as I watched him looking at me and weighing his decision. What was the right thing to do? It was actually pretty disconcerting. But I still trusted him.

Finally one Sunday, he asked to meet with me again following sacrament meeting. I was nervous. What would he say? What had he decided? As we sat down together, he told me that after much consideration and prayer, he believed I had fully repented and was now ready to move forward.

I was grateful and relieved. I now felt forgiven both by God and by the Church. I saw both as a necessary part of the process. The bishop told me that he would think about a calling for me in the ward and that in time, we would discuss my return to the temple. That was more than I could have hoped for. I wanted to hug him. And maybe I did.

A few weeks before that meeting with my bishop, I was in a sacrament meeting with Brent where he related the story of the prodigal son to a congregation of people that included both my children and my granddaughter. Brent began by saying that he had always seen himself in that particular story as the good brother who stayed home. Made sense to me. That's how I'd always seen him too.

But he surprised me as he went on to say that he was wrong about that. He was not the good brother who stayed home. He too was a prodigal son. That we were all prodigal sons and daughters in need of Christ's atonement and the Lord's tender mercies. He went on to say that we had all fallen short and were in need of the love and forgiveness of a kind and loving Father. That one day when we returned to His presence, He would see us coming from afar off and fall on our necks and weep with joy.

Rather than resenting my return to the Church and the joy with which it had been greeted by others, as the "good brother" had in the story of the prodigal son, my brother Brent generously aligned himself with me and declared himself also to be a prodigal son. And he put everyone else in the congregation on the same footing, such that I felt neither lost nor alone. Brent was truly the leader/servant that day in my eyes. I had done nothing to deserve such generosity and love. But I was filled with such a sense of appreciation, that I could scarcely contain it.

I was not the only one moved by his words. So were Alicia, Alex, and Jenna. My mom, my brothers and their families were all sitting next to us on the same benches. We were weeping openly as a family, our hearts knit together in love. We found that we didn't have nearly enough tissues to go around.

# XXII

## Saying Good-bye

Our family clan was gathering to say good-bye. The winds of change had quite unexpectedly blown us all off course, as winds of change seem to do. This weekend marked our last time together as an extended family in Twin Falls—the family focal point now for more than 25 years. A month ago, my mom moved to Salt Lake City to be closer to Dave and Norm. Next month, Brent was leaving his law practice behind, and he and Marcia were moving first to Salt Lake for a year, and then off to parts unknown. The whole world seemed tipsy turvy.

After flying to Salt Lake and spending the night with Dave, I drove Mom to Twin Falls. It was a beautiful June summer day for a drive, and it was just the two of us. We had hours to talk. The unexpected move had been hard on her, so we talked a lot about that. It wasn't easy making that kind of adjustment at 85. But today, she was happy just to be going back home. It didn't seem long before we passed through the familiar rolling green hills and crossed the border into Idaho.

A few hours later, we found ourselves on the Perrine Bridge, crossing over the Snake River Canyon into Twin Falls. I dropped Mom off at the local Diary Queen to spend some time with her friend Carolyn. It was their favorite haunt to talk over ice cream. Then I drove out to Brent and Marcia's. It was strange to think that this would be our last weekend together here, after all the holidays, picnics, and reunions we'd had in Twin Falls. It was the end of an era for our family.

As I pulled up the drive to the house and got out of the car, nieces, nephews, grandnieces, and grand nephews came running out of the house for hugs. I felt so warm and welcomed. Lucy was especially happy to see me. "Sue-sue, Sue-sue," she shouted as she climbed into my arms and again laid her head on my shoulder. There is absolutely nothing that compares to the hug of a child who loves you.

Brent was standing in the driveway, getting the family boat ready to sell. So even the boat was going. We'd all had fun times out on the boat. The eager buyers soon pulled up in front. It was a single mom with her two teenage sons. After watching them together, I was sure they'd love the boat. Brent was giving them the water skis and life jackets. Those boys were so excited.

After papers were signed and money exchanged, we all just stood out on the lawn and watched in disbelief as they drove the boat away. And then Marcia burst into tears. I gave her my best sister-in-law hug. This was the end of an era for her family too. It wasn't how she'd either pictured it or planned for it all these years. Brent and Marcia would now be serving the Church full-time.

We ate dinner that night at Brent's. Then we drove over to Mom's old house so she could take a look at the place. Mom hadn't seen her house since she'd left it so abruptly in May. As we opened the front door to the house, I wondered how my mom would feel being back inside. Her house had been transformed. The familiar wall paper was gone, replaced by white paint. The powder blue carpets had been pulled out and exchanged for a neutral brown color. The kitchen had faux wood flooring. Mom started to cry. She owned the house, but it just wasn't home anymore.

Katy and Tyler were renting the house from Mom for the time being. While they hadn't moved in yet, most of their furniture was there. We walked around the rooms, and Katy showed us where their furniture was going. I was frankly relieved when Alicia and Jenna called to say they were just pulling in to the hotel. So we said goodbye for the time being to Mom's old house and Katy's new house and locked the door behind us. Then we drove to the Hampton Inn to meet Alicia and Jenna. It turned out to be a late night.

The next morning was Saturday. Alex and Karry drove into town and went straight to Brent's. It was fun to see Karry again. I smiled knowingly since I knew that Karry wasn't aware that a few weeks from now, when we would be in Lake Tahoe together, Alex was going to propose. Alicia and I knew, but we were careful not to mention it to Jenna. She was likely to get so excited that she'd spill the beans.

There were almost 40 of us in the house for dinner that night, counting the little guys. After dessert, the little babies went to bed and the rest of us moved out to the backyard for smores and a fire. The kids loved eating the gooey marshmallows stuck in between squares of chocolate. Alex and my niece Emily's husband Jeff were the master toasters. I had one or two of the perfectly browned marshmallows. Whenever the fire burned down, Marcia took the wood she had chopped herself and tossed it onto the burning embers. No Presto logs for that girl!

When it began to grow dark, the next round of children went to bed. Now it was just the adults. We pulled our chairs into a circle around the fire and started talking about campfire memories. I told my nieces and nephews that I'd grown up going to girl's camp and making fires. I'd even gone winter camping one time in the snow. They laughed and found it hard to believe. But it was true just the same.

Then my brother Dave suggested that since our nephew Dave was leaving on his mission soon, it might be fun to go around the circle and share our favorite "little Dave memories," even though Dave wasn't so little anymore. All of us but Dave, who would be the center of attention, thought that was a great idea. He was quickly overruled. Each of us came up with the funniest Dave story we could think of, the next one trying to outdo the one who had gone before.

We were laughing one minute and crying the next. Even the men. We tried desperately to hold onto the moment as long as we could. I thought about the shadows of past family campfires and cool summer evenings we'd shared together in Twin Falls. I was going to miss this place.

The next day was Sunday. Brent, Marcia, and their son Dave were speaking in sacrament meeting. Today they would be saying good-bye to their ward family. My nephew Dave spoke first. His talk quite simply took my breath away. His gospel knowledge was, in a word, profound. I kept wondering who this young man was who was addressing us in this manner. It was certainly not the boy we'd told stories about around the campfire the night before. Dave spoke with a power and conviction that was way beyond his 19 years. Alicia and Alex thought so too.

After Brent delivered his moving talk on the prodigal son, and the tearful meeting concluded, we went back to Brent and Marcia's for one final meal. Our time together was growing short. In a few hours we'd all be going our separate ways, making the drive back to different locations. After more than 25 years, our Twin time was almost behind us.

When we got back to Brent's, my nephew Dave came up and gave me a big hug. I think losing the family home, just prior to flying off to Japan for two years on his mission, was harder on him than it was on anyone else. With tears running down his face, Dave told me how much he loved me. He said he was sad I hadn't been able to go through the temple with him the day before. He said when he got back from Japan, he wanted to go through the temple just with me. I promised him I'd be ready, waiting, and anxious for us to go through the temple together.

After dinner ended, we knelt and prayed together as a family for the safety of all those who would be traveling that day. So this is it, I thought. This is good-bye. People started trickling out the door, reluctantly. Mom and I were two of the last to go.

Alicia and Jenna were on their way back to St. George. Alex and Karry to Southern California. Mom and I were driving back to Salt Lake, as were Norm and Dave, many of their children, and Brent's children. I was relieved and grateful when everyone arrived safely home. While it was true that we didn't have a place to gather in Twin Falls anymore, we would always have each other, together forever. No one could take that away from us.

# XXIII

## As If You Had Never Left

*I* had a business conference scheduled in Los Angeles the last week in June. I'd made my flight arrangements months ago, so I could spend the weekend prior with Alex and Karry in Orange County. Then Brent called to tell me he was coming to San Clemente the same weekend. "I thought you were going to Redfish with your family," I said, surprised.

"That was the plan," he answered. "But I've decided to leave early. I've been asked to speak in the San Clemente stake conference. Do you think Alex and Karry might want to come?"

"I'm pretty sure they would. And, as it happens, I'll be in town that weekend. So I'd like to come too."

"Really? The same weekend?!" Brent said. "Can you come both Saturday night and Sunday?"

"I can. Absolutely. I think Alex and Karry have a wedding to go to Saturday night. But I'm sure they'll want to come Sunday."

My next thought was to call Mark and Kate Boud. I hadn't seen them for a few years now, but they'd already heard through the grapevine that I was back in the Church. They'd waited a long time for me to find my way back. I told them I'd be in San Clemente for conference Saturday night and wondered if they'd be free for dinner. "Are you kidding?!" Mark said. "We wouldn't miss it."

I was also looking forward to seeing my old friend Bishop Reese, who was now the president of the San Clemente stake. I'd spoken with his wife Diane a few weeks earlier, so Curtis knew I had returned to the Church. I'm not typically anxious to tell people that they were right and

I was wrong. But this time I was. I wanted to let Curtis know he was right about me returning to the Church.

When I arrived at the Boud home, Mark was already over at the stake center saving seats. Mark and Kate had decided the best plan would be to pick up dinner and bring it to the stake center.

As we ate, Mark and Kate wanted more details about what had brought me back to the Church after being gone for so long. I told them what I could piece together in half an hour. It was difficult to fully describe either my feelings or the events that had transpired in any kind of linear or logical fashion, since there wasn't anything linear or logical about it.

After we finished dinner, Mark, Kate and I walked into the cultural hall. We hadn't been in our seats long before Brent came up to say hello and meet Mark and Kate. He remarked to me as we walked out of the room what a really a great couple they were. He had no idea.

I went next to the stake president's office to see Curtis Reese. When Curtis saw me coming, he reached forward and embraced me. Tears welled up in both our eyes as we smiled into each other's faces. "You told me I'd come back one day, Curtis. And you were right."

Curtis graciously did not say "I told you so." He just hugged me happily.

As we waited for the meeting to begin, I thought about all the time I'd been away. About all the things I'd missed. How would I ever make up for all that lost time? The question made me sad, because I knew I simply couldn't.

One of the speakers was someone who was also coming back to the Church. He'd been gone 40 years. He bore his testimony, and with tears in his eyes told the congregation that his brother was coming tomorrow to ordain him an elder. He spoke about how glad he was to be back in the Church. I cried quietly, knowing just how he felt. It was similar to losing my health and then getting it back again. It felt so good. I never wanted to take my faith for granted again.

Then Brent spoke about the lost sheep and read from Luke: "And which of you, having lost a sheep, will not leave the ninety and nine and go after the one. And when you have found it, you lift it upon your shoulders and carry it home." Then he described how the Shepherd called all his neighbors and family together to rejoice with him over the return of his lost sheep. Brent said that's how God and the Savior feel when one of their own comes home.

What an amazing thing that is, I thought. Rather than criticizing people for being gone, for whatever their reason, the idea was instead to rejoice over their return.

After the meeting ended, I saw so many old friends—people I hadn't seen in years. One of them sobbed happily. Another one kept saying, "I love you, Susan." And still another commented on the "glow" he saw on my face. They were just the same as the people in Luke. These very good friends with their very tender hearts, rejoicing over my return to the Church. My joy was full.

The next morning, I attended a meeting with new members, investigators, and anyone who'd been newly reactivated. I wasn't sure in the beginning that I wanted to go. I was frankly embarrassed about being newly reactivated. But Brent convinced me I should go, so I did.

The visiting authority addressed each group's needs individually. He first asked any new members to raise their hands. He counseled them to be patient. He said that the Church was not a mausoleum for saints, but a laboratory where good people were learning every day to become better. He said that some people in the Church might not seem to be all that they should be, and that new members shouldn't be disturbed by that.

Next he asked the investigators to raise their hands. There were quite a few. He told the investigators how anxious we were to share what we had with them. And that if we seemed too anxious at times, it was only because our faith meant so much to us.

Only one group to go now. The inactives. That was my group. It was clear that I was going to have to raise my hand. There was no getting around it. I wished I could just pretend I'd never left.

"Are there any here who've been gone from the Church and are now coming back?" he asked. I didn't want to be the person who'd left the Church. But I was. And I was sitting right up front. So I raised my hand. There were two other people besides me, so at least I wasn't completely alone. He then told us in no uncertain terms that there was nothing worth leaving the Church over. Ever. He's right about that, I thought. Faith is a choice that's worth making. And I regretted that I'd chosen doubt for so long instead.

And then he said something unexpected, "I give you a blessing that the things you knew about the gospel and the things that you understood previously will all be restored to you. And it will be as if you never left." Then he welcomed us back.

I was stunned. He had spoken to the exact concerns of my heart. Thoughts that I'd shared with no one but my Heavenly Father. It was hard to take it all in, so I just sat there numb, unable or unwilling to move. When others started getting up, I walked automatically after them, still thinking about what we'd just been promised.

Seats had been reserved up front for those of us who attended the early meeting, so I saved seats next to me for Alex and Karry. I was so glad to see them when they came in through the side door and sat down by me. Alex asked me right away if I were ok. I told him I'd tell him later.

It wasn't long before choir and congregation rose together to sing the opening song. More than a thousand resonant voices surrounded me, singing, "Now Let Us Rejoice." When we got to the part "no longer as strangers on earth need we roam," tears began running down my face. I wanted so much to sing, but I couldn't, as the Spirit reminded me of what I'd known and learned all my life. A new light was filling my mind and heart.

It was at that moment that I finally understood the concept of pure intelligence. That was how my perspective shifted so suddenly. That was how I woke up, as it were. That was how I'd been pulled through a worm hole in my universe. One thing I knew beyond any shadow of a doubt: It wasn't my intelligence that had made it happen. I knew exactly what my intelligence looked like at work. And this was not it.

Then Brent spoke. He talked about how the added ballast of living a Christ-centered life serves to keep our lives on track, much as adding weight to the back of a truck prevents it from slipping off the road in icy weather. He quoted Matthew 11:28–29. "Come unto me all ye that are heavy laden, and I will give you rest. Take my yoke upon you, and learn of me; for I am meek and lowly in heart: and ye shall find rest unto your souls." It was at this moment that Karry decided to begin investigating the Church. She was tired of bearing her burdens alone.

The visiting authority spoke next and told a story about his sons when they were little. He described how one of them had been injured when his "Hot Wheels" tricycle hit a car. He'd scraped his arm and face. His brother, who was just a few years older than he was, took him into the house, washed his wound, and covered it with Neosporin and bandages. Getting patched up felt so good to him that he went out and offered Neosporin and band aids to all the neighbors.

Then he said, "That's why we want to share the gospel with you. We've had our wounds cleaned and bound, and it feels so good, we want you to feel the same thing. So don't be offended if we seem overly anxious to share the gospel with you." Alex particularly loved that story.

After conference ended, Alex, Karry, and I walked outside together. The adult leaders were preparing lunch for the youth of the stake. Alex had his own reunion with former young men leaders and scout leaders, who'd helped him earn merit badges and gone with him on 50-mile hikes. We spent an hour catching up and talking with old friends and neighbors. It was a sweet moment for Alex. Karry was impressed with the sense of community we shared with each other. And everyone loved Karry.

I received a burning testimony that day that the Lord is in the details of each of our spiritual lives, if we will just let him in. I knew without question that it was no coincidence Brent, Alex, Karry and I were all together that day in San Clemente. As President Reese said later, quoting Oliver Cowdery, "these are days never to be forgotten." He was right. For my part, I felt similar to Ammon when he said, " . . . yea, we will rejoice, for our joy is full . . . I cannot say the smallest part which I feel."

My wounds had been cleaned and bound. It was in Orange County where my life came apart in my hands 14 years before. And it was in Orange County where the Lord glued it all back together and gave it to me again.

# XIV

# The "Double-dog Dare"

*T*here was a lot I had to do before I could return to the temple. For me, the most challenging was going to be paying my tithing. Probably because it involved parting with my money. That sounded particularly painful. Could I really do this, I wondered? Could I even afford to give 10% of my income to the Church?

Ok, yes, I could afford it. I could pay my tithing and still have more to live on than I'd had 2 years ago. But I still wasn't particularly happy about it. For the past 14 years, money, and the accumulation of it, had steadily become more important to me.

It was apparent that I was going to need help coming to terms with the principle of paying tithing again. So once more I spoke with Brent. When I had concerns or questions, I called Brent and Marcia. They patiently spent many long hours with me either on the phone or in person, helping me resolve my questions.

When I shared my fears with Brent over paying tithing, his response was wholly unexpected. Instead of giving me a litany of reasons why I should pay my tithing, he simply said that the Lord hadn't missed my money in my absence. That wasn't the response I'd expected. "Really?" I queried.

"No. We didn't miss your money, Susan. Think about how much the Church has prospered and grown since you've been gone. When you left, there were about 9 million members of the Church. Now there are in excess of 13 million members."

"Wow. I had no idea," I said. "4 million more members."

"That's right," Brent continued. "The Church continues to grow, Susan. And the Lord doesn't need your money to do it." I was relieved there for just a split second. Maybe I wouldn't have to pay my tithing after all.

After having said that the Lord didn't need my money, Brent went on, "But you need the blessings that will come into your life from paying your tithing, Susan."

Then he asked me if I knew about the Lord's "double-dog dare" scripture. "There's a double-dog dare, scripture?" I asked incredulously. "Now I know you're joking," I said, thinking back to the double-dog dares of our childhood that found me leaping out of tree houses and into snow banks.

"Actually, I'm not," he replied. "There's only one place in all of the scriptures where the Lord says: 'Prove me now herewith.' And it's in Malachi. It's the ultimate challenge scripture, Susan. Malachi 3: 10 says: "Bring ye all the tithes into the storehouse, that there may be meat in mine house, and prove me now herewith, saith the Lord of hosts, if I will not open you the windows of heaven, and pour you out a blessing, that there shall not be room enough to receive it."

I had to admit that was a pretty powerful promise. "But, Brent," I said. "I know people who pay their tithing who don't have much money."

"It's not just about the money, Susan," he replied patiently. "Prosperity can also mean having a close family, enjoying good health, having a clear mind, or even growing spiritually."

Brent was right. There had to be more important things in life than money. Ever since the world had fallen into a global recession, I'd spent an amazing amount of time thinking and worrying about my money. I asked myself the same questions over and over: Should I reinvest in the stock market? If so, when? Or should I just hide my money under my mattress?

Every day when I got up in the morning, before I did anything else, I turned on the television and watched "Squawk on the Street." I followed the markets. I poured over the economic news. I worried. And then I worried some more. Would things get worse?

Now my brother Brent was suggesting that I do the scariest and riskiest thing of all, in my mind: Pay my tithing. Give 10% of my income to the Church. The ultimate challenge. I decided it was too late in my life to start turning down double-dog dares now.

So I took the leap of faith and began paying my tithing. Writing the first check wasn't too painful. Writing the second was more challenging than writing the first. But it got easier with each check. I always paid my tithing first.

Eventually, I noticed that I could still do what I needed and wanted to do, even when I was paying my tithing. In fact, after I had paid my tithing for several months, I wondered what I used to do with that money before I gave it to the Lord.

An important part of my increase was now going to help others. It was being used for the Lord's purposes to build and maintain temples and meetinghouses, to sustain missionary work, to educate other members of the Church. My money was spreading itself around out there, doing good for others. I liked the way that made me feel.

One day when I was on a business trip, at the end of an unusually tiring day, I opened my hotel bible to Luke chapter 12. Christ was relating a parable. He described a man who was enlarging his property and building bigger barns so he could be comfortable for the rest of his life. But that night, his "soul was required of him" and he died. Then what did his preparations matter? He was dead. And he obviously couldn't take it with him.

It became evident why it might be difficult for people to have too much money. It seemed that the more I had, the more I thought I needed. I read on in Luke 12, "Where your treasure is, there will your heart be also."

My heart had become too set on my financial well being and not enough on what mattered most. I needed to be thinking more about enlarging my soul, rather than my 401-K. Thinking more about serving others, lightening hearts, lifting up the arms that hang down. Being the Lord's servant. I needed to use my time and money to bless the lives of others. What did it profit me, if I gained the whole world and lost my own soul?

So in addition to paying my tithing, I stopped watching "Squawk on the Street" in the morning and "Cramer" at night. Instead, I determined to just set it and forget it, when it came to my money. I reread my patriarchal blessing again, which counseled me to: "Live each day for the joy of living, for the service you can give to others wherever you go." And it reminded me to, "Spread sunshine and hope."

I'd done precious little of that in quite some time, I thought. Instead, I'd made it all about me. Without realizing it, I had become very self-focused. So I tried instead to spread more sunshine in the lives of others. And I found that as I lost my life, I found it again.

I was happier. My children were doing better. I was closer to my family. I was even more focused at work. The rest of that year was one of the best years I'd had in a long time.

As I moved into the next year, my boss, who is not a believer, found out from one of my colleagues that I'd returned to my faith. It surprised him. He asked me one night over dinner, "How do you think going back to your church has affected your performance as an employee?"

I responded as respectfully and frankly as I could, "You tell me. You just wrote in my performance review that I had the best year of my career. You gave me my full bonus. How do you think my return to my faith has affected my performance as an employee?"

"I thought it all had to do with my great mentoring," he chuckled.

"There's no doubt that your great mentoring has had a positive impact on me," I assured him. "But returning to my faith has made me feel more settled, more focused, more congruent. It's made me a better person and a better employee." He couldn't argue with that. For my part, I just knew that believing that my life was guided by the hand of providence rather than believing that it was ruled by chance was a particularly happy change for me.

The Lord had poured out abundant blessings in my life that I believed were the direct result of my willingness to at last be obedient, to pay my tithing, and to accept his challenge to "prove him now herewith." I had. And he had come through for me. My life had been blessed in ways that I could not have imagined the month I first began paying my tithing. And now, I simply cannot afford not to.

# XV

# Maintaining Change

*I* was shocked to find that, after the deeply moving experiences I'd had over the past few months, I could still face challenges to my growing testimony. But I did. My most serious challenge came in the form of debilitating comments from an otherwise good friend, who was still inactive in the Church. I had suspected that my return to the Church would prove difficult for her. I'd delayed telling her I was going back, because I had anticipated her response.

Even so, I was not prepared for the tenor of the attacks. She hit me where it hurt. Comments such as, "Your intellect has shrunk and you are now capable only of shallow conversations." That ridiculous and impossible statement made me angry. She in effect called me stupid because I was once again a believer But her words had the desired effect: a small doubt niggled itself into the back of my mind.

Later she accused me of not being able to think for myself because I would obviously now, in her mind, follow the prophet blindly. I found her old Anti-Mormon rhetoric so tiring. Inside I sighed deeply. Did she not remember that as a people, Mormons have always been directed to receive their own confirmation of revelation?

I think former president and prophet Wilford Woodruff said it best: "the gift of the Holy Ghost is the greatest gift that can be bestowed upon man . . . It is not restricted to men, nor to apostles or prophets; it belongs to every faithful man and woman, and to every child who is old enough to receive the gospel of Christ." It wouldn't have helped to remind her that the gift of the Holy Ghost was everyone's province, not just the prophet's. So I didn't.

A few weeks later, she asked me to tell her what it was that had brought me back to the Church. I thought she was honestly curious and sincerely wanted to know. I shared my experiences with her as frankly as I could, thinking it might help her understand my decision better. As I talked about what had changed my heart, I could literally see smirks of disbelief curl the corners of her mouth. I was sorry at once that I'd been so forthcoming.

The next day came the attacking email. I was caught off guard by her level of anger. She said that I had returned to the Church because I lacked courage and had to belong to something. As if belonging to a community of faith was a cowardly thing to do. She went on to say that I had now "sunk into boredom and commonality."

She accused me of instability and inconsistency—two things that I didn't want to be, along with stupid, of course. She said that I had "bounced back" into the Church because it was a convenient time to do so. She declared that she no longer knew who I was. I, on the other hand, thought I was more like myself now than I'd been in a very long time.

She discounted what were for me spiritual promptings and said that I had just gotten tired of being different and had to belong to something again. And then finally, she told me that my actions had changed our friendship forever. That was devastating to hear.

But I didn't want to doubt what I couldn't deny. Believing in the sacred had brought me great happiness and peace. As I regained my faith, I had become more optimistic. More hopeful. More connected. More outwardly focused. Rather than my experiences contracting who I was, my mind and soul expanded. I now had the twin tools of both reason and revelation at my disposal.

Reading my friend's email would regrettably not be my last dark moment or my last temptation to return to old friends and habits that, while familiar and perhaps comfortable, were not taking me in the direction I wanted to go.

As my desire grew to go back to the temple, the doubt and darkness seemed to mount. One particularly troubling night, I awoke from a disturbing nightmare that I couldn't even remember. I only knew how it made me feel. And it wasn't good.

All the next day I was plagued with fear and questions. That evening,

Brent and Marcia called to see how I was doing. I was so happy to hear their voices. We spent a few hours together on the phone.

As we talked, Marcia remembered a devotional address Elder Holland had given at BYU in 1999, titled, "Cast Not Away Therefore Your Confidence." Marcia pulled up his talk on her computer and read me these words: "Beware the temptation to retreat from a good thing. If it was right when you prayed about it and trusted it and lived for it, it is right now." Those were exactly the words I needed to hear.

Even before we got off the phone, Marcia emailed me a link to Elder Holland's talk, which I subsequently downloaded and printed. I read it both that night and for many nights to come. Elder Holland also cautioned: "Don't assume that a great revelation, some marvelous illuminating moment, the opening of some inspired path, is the end of it." He went on to say, "I wish to encourage every one of us regarding the opposition that so often comes after enlightened decisions have been made, after moments of revelation and conviction have given us a peace and an assurance we thought we would never lose."

That's exactly what I had mistakenly believed: That the peace and assurance I had received would never leave me. Not ever. Not for a moment. I was so surprised to be having feelings of doubt, fear, and worry, even occasionally.

I'd been sailing along for the past several months on an amazing spiritual journey. I now knew things both in my mind and my heart. I'd been imbued with a spirit of peace. In my happiness, I seemed to have forgotten that a trial of faith is typically part of the process. I hadn't factored in the certainty that I would face opposition from more than one someone and more than one something.

Elder Holland went on to offer these words of hope: "The light will come again. The darkness will retreat. The safety will be sure. Stay the course and see the beauty of life unfold before you." I loved that last bit, "See the beauty of life unfold before you."

I decided I was meant to move with all speed to prepare myself to return to the temple. If I retreated from my resolve now, the opportunity might never come to me in this way again. I was in a special time and place with a given purpose. The place was here and the time was now. I kept Elder Holland's talk in my night stand by my bed and read it often, until the print on the pages began to smudge.

After that night's conversation with Brent and Marcia, Marcia wrote me an email. I printed it and taped it in my journal. "I have never believed that you didn't believe, Susan. To me, it is just who you are. It has been almost impossible for me to believe that you left the Church behind, and I have always, always believed that you would be back. The Lord allows us to figure a lot of things out for ourselves. I love you, Susan. I love you in or out of the Church. I hope you know that." And I did know that. I always had.

Marcia was right. A Mormon is who I am. And a Mormon is who I've always been, whether I've continuously chosen to acknowledge it to myself or not. Coming back did not mean that I wasn't smart or courageous. Quite the contrary. Mormons are some of the most educated, courageous, and organized people I know in the world.

Somewhere along the line, I'd lost my way. I stopped believing and stopped associating with the saints. I thought foolishly that faith was the enemy of reason. As a result, I found myself always searching, never complete, and never fully centered. I was separated from my family and my culture. It brought me no lasting happiness.

One summer evening, I again found myself filled with fear and many "what ifs." What had happened to my faith and confidence? This intense level of fear and negativity was unusual for me at any stage of my life, in or out of the Church. I shared my feelings with one of my new friends. She listened carefully and then said, "Susan, your job is just to move forward in faith. Trust the Lord to open the doors."

Trust the Lord, she had said. Maybe I could remember how to do that. This was the same advice my Grandmother Hatch had given all her grandchildren over and over when we were growing up, quoting Proverbs. "Trust in the Lord with all thine heart and lean not unto thine own understanding. In all thy ways acknowledge him, and he shall direct thy paths." I prayed that he would, and I leaned on my family and friends in the Church for support.

# XVI

# Shall We Not Go On . . . ?

One Sunday in mid-August, I asked the bishop if I could speak with him after sacrament meeting. He told me he'd been just about to ask me if I would meet with him. I wondered what it was he wanted to say to me. I knew exactly what I wanted to say to him. I wanted to ask him what I had to do to go back to the temple. I was again trying to move forward with faith. I hoped the Lord was ready to open this particular door for me.

After sacrament meeting, I made my way to the bishop's office. As we sat down together, he suggested that I go first. Why did I want to meet with him? I asked him what it would take for me to get ready to return to the temple. "Interesting," he said. "I wanted to meet with you to ask you about taking the temple preparation class." The door was open.

"I'd appreciate the opportunity to take the class," I responded. When does it start?"

"I don't have an exact start date in mind," he smiled. "I still need to call a teacher. But soon."

"Do you have a manual on hand that I could look at in the meantime?" I asked eagerly. He searched his cabinets, but he didn't have one right there in his office.

"I'll get you one," he promised.

Then I asked, "Do you think I could be ready to go back to the temple by early October?"

"Wow. It's almost the end of August. I'm not sure if you can be ready that soon, Susan," he said. "Why October?"

"I'm going to Salt Lake for conference. My whole family will be there, and it would be wonderful if we could attend a session together," I replied.

Having said that, I still wasn't exactly sure why October seemed all that important. It might be a convenient time. But it's not as if my whole family wouldn't show up whenever and wherever I went back to the temple.

"I'll have to think about it, Susan," Bishop Sopp replied gently. I knew he saw this as a big step. I'd been gone from the temple for a long time. There needed to be no question in either of our minds that I was ready to renew my covenants.

Then to my mind came the words, "Ask him if there's anything standing in the way of your return to the temple." Ok, I thought. I was growing more accustomed to this kind of spiritual direction. It wasn't as surprising as it had been 4 months ago, but it was still sometimes disconcerting. So I asked the bishop the exact question I'd been prompted to ask.

He thought for a moment. "No," he answered. There's nothing standing in the way of your return to the temple. Let me see what I can do." I thanked him, shook his hand, and left.

That afternoon, Merrill Hales called and asked me to join the temple preparation class the next Sunday. He told me he'd be teaching it. I guess the bishop had found his teacher. I was so glad it would be Merrill.

The next Sunday, the talks in sacrament meeting turned out to be all about the temple. It amazed me how I went to church every week and heard just exactly what I needed to know and understand at that particular point in time. I was thankful for these tender mercies.

Our visiting high councilor spoke about the blessings of temple service. He based some of his message on a talk Elder Scott had given titled: "Temple Service: Source of Strength and Power in a Time of Need." My favorite line from Elder Scott's talk was "conversion is when your heart tells you something your mind does not know." This from a man who'd spent his career as a nuclear physicist. No one could ever credibly tell me again that religion was for the weak minded.

Elder Scott's statement expressed perfectly for me what happened as I was moved upon by the Spirit to come back to the Church. It wasn't my mind that upended my paradigm; it was the Spirit speaking to my heart. It was difficult in the beginning for my mind to grasp that my heart knew something for which reason alone could not provide an answer. I was grateful I could now see with both my mind and my heart.

When the meeting ended, I went to my first temple preparation class. There were two of us in the class. Merrill spoke to us of the importance of covenants and consecration. My remembrance of temple blessings came quickly back to me. I recalled the essential nature of the covenants I'd made in the temple and then later set at naught. I reminded myself that when someone makes a promise to me, I expect that promise to be honored. And yet I had made promises in the temple that I did not keep.

I'd been raised to believe that honorable people kept their promises. Acting dishonorably had not brought me joy. So I was glad for the opportunity to once more prove myself to be an honorable person, capable of both making and keeping covenants and promises.

That night I drove down the hill to the Mormon Center to hear the Sacramento temple matron speak about the temple. I'd met Sister Winkle a few months prior at a stake high priest's group dinner. When she heard I was getting ready to go back to the temple, she said, "The temple is for you, Susan. Please come and find me the day you come back." I promised her I would.

Among the other things Sister Winkle told us, she said: "You've been prayed into the temple by your ancestors, some of whom are still waiting." My thoughts turned to the Nielson line. But so many people in my family had done genealogy. I thought we'd pretty much exhausted most of the possibilities. But tonight, I wondered, had we? I made a mental note to call my cousin Judith to see if she had any ideas where I might begin looking.

On my way to work the next day, I was again filled with unexpected and unexplained fears. I was both exhausted and troubled by the extreme swings between strong spiritual feelings and my own anxiety, doubt, and skepticism. I found myself attempting to climb over unseen barriers. I was sure the temple was my end goal, and I still knew that for whatever reason, it needed to be October. But some days, it just wasn't easy trying to get myself there.

A few days later, Norm, Dave, and I got an email from Brent. He told us the Church was training him on the new Family Search program, which was being introduced in Utah. As part of his training, Brent had been asked in June which family line he wanted to research. He had decided on the Nielson line.

The morning Brent sent his email, a specialist in both Swedish and Danish genealogy from the Family History Department met with Brent in his office. She had found that our Great-Grandmother Sophia had a brother Christopher who'd remained behind in Sweden when she married and moved to Denmark. Christopher and his family's temple work had never been done. Brent wrote, "I was thinking that when Susan is ready to go to the temple, we could all go together and take the family names the researcher is finding for us."

Typing through tears, I hit reply all and let my family know I was working to be ready to go to the temple by October 5, the Monday following General Conference.

Two days later, I completed my final day of the temple preparation class. Merrill reiterated that going to the temple and making covenants was a serious commitment not to be entered into lightly. As I listened, I checked in with myself to make sure I was fully ready to take this step. I knew there would be no way to ever again maintain my sense of personal integrity if I didn't keep my covenants this time.

I was expending my agency in making this one, single choice. There would never be space to go back and revisit this decision. Bishop Sopp quoted David O. McKay that day: "Spirituality is the consciousness of victory over self and communion with the infinite." It had been a wonderful Sunday.

In stark contrast, the next day was another black Monday. I couldn't believe it. This particular black Monday persisted through most of the week. My faith and confidence again fled. Fear filled my mind. What if you're not ready to go back to the temple? I asked myself. What if you fail? How could I make the questions stop? I wondered. I took comfort in knowing that I'd be spending the upcoming Labor Day weekend in Salt Lake with my mother, brothers, and cousins.

I flew in to Salt Lake Friday night, and Dave picked me up at the airport. We drove to his home, where I collected Mom's overnight bag and added my own to the trunk of her car. We were soon on our way to the little Swiss town of Midway. My cousin Nancy and her husband John had invited us up to their chalet to have dinner and spend the night. I was looking forward to a quiet night in the mountains.

It turned out to be a lovely evening in an incredible setting. Nancy, Mom, and I talked and talked over dinner. John arrived late, and as we sat around the large fire in the living room, Nancy asked me to recount what it was that had brought me back to the Church. It felt good to describe the events and my associated feelings. It reminded me why I was doing what I was doing.

When it was finally time for bed, I happily climbed up the stairs to the dormer room. I slept peacefully that night under the heavy quilt. The cool mountain air caressed my face and whispered through my hair. I was at peace. I was thankful for supportive cousins and the chance to just be still.

The next morning, we thanked Nancy and John for their hospitality and told them good-bye. We drove down the mountain so we could meet Brent and Marcia for lunch. After lunch, Mom went home to rest and Marcia and I walked around Temple Square together. I asked her if we could go over to the Joseph Smith Building and watch the film on the restoration. She was happy to do that with me.

As we watched the movie, I connected to the unfolding events. I'd been studying and reading about Joseph Smith again. Yes there was controversy in his life. But, I asked myself, what spiritual or historical leader had there ever been anywhere at any time whose life was not touched by controversy from someone's perspective?

I'd decided that there was so much more to recommend itself about Joseph Smith's life and mission and the Book of Mormon than there was to be concerned about. Brent also suggested that I trust my ancestors, trust my family who had been with Joseph Smith in the very beginning, trust in those who believed in him and in what he was doing. There's no doubt that the restoration of the Church was part of my family's history, tradition, and faith.

As the film ended, Joseph Smith uttered the words, "Shall we not go on in so great a cause?" When I heard those words, I started sobbing. And I knew I had my answer. I wanted to return to the temple. As everyone else filed out of the theatre, Marcia sat there with me and just held my hand while I collected myself. She didn't know what had touched me. And she didn't care at the moment.

When I was ready, we left the building and walked out into the fading sunshine. We sat outside on a bench, and I poured my heart out to her. And then she poured her heart out to me. As we cried together, the Salt Lake temple rose to our left; the sun glinted off its tall spires and then skipped across the quiet reflecting pond.

And that was it. The conflict was over. The darkness dispelled and did not return.

# XVII

# You Are Home Now, You Know

*I* was on my way back to Sacramento. When my brother Dave dropped me off at the airport, he gave me one of his full-on hugs. "I love you, Susan," he smiled warmly. "Have a safe flight home."

"I love you too, Dave," I hugged back. "Thanks for being such a good brother. And thanks for letting me stay with you and Jaci . . . again."

"You're welcome anytime," he grinned. "You know that." Then he handed me a package. "We thought you might enjoy these Michael Wilcox CDs on the temple."

"For me? Thanks, Dave. There's nothing I'd rather have right now." And I reached up and hugged him again.

Then with tears standing on his blue, blue eyes Dave said, "I'm so proud of you, Susan." It meant everything to hear my baby brother tell me he was proud of me.

After I got home, I put the CDs in my car, and I listened to them more than once, usually on my way driving back and forth to work. It helped me refocus my thoughts on what would be most important to me when I went back to the temple.

As I listened, I thought about the early saints—my ancestors among them—and I was struck by how much they'd sacrificed to build those first temples. They'd given up everything they had. The women of the Kirtland temple even crushed up precious china they'd brought with them from England to add luster to the outer walls. And they did it with willing and happy hearts. I marveled at how the power of faith makes seemingly impossible things possible.

The next Sunday I had my temple recommend interview with the bishop. I was ready. I knew the questions, and I was confident in my answers. I had a faith and surety that had come from the exit of my own refiner's fire. Bishop Sopp found me worthy to return to the temple, and he happily signed my first temple recommend in 15 years. I tucked it carefully away in a special corner of my wallet.

The bishop suggested that I attend the temple in Sacramento before going through a session with my family in Salt Lake in October. "It might be easier for you to focus on the work you're doing with your family, if you become familiar again with the ordinances of the temple," he advised. Made sense.

So over the next few weeks, I went to the temple twice. Sister Winkle was in the temple the second time and so, as I had promised, I went to her office and found her. She was thrilled to see me. In fact, everyone serving in the Sacramento temple was happy to see me. People who had never met me nodded, smiled fondly, and said things such as, "Welcome to the temple." They seemed genuinely pleased that I was there.

Sister Winkle took me to the bride's room. In the middle of the room hangs a large portrait of Queen Esther. It's a beautiful original oil painting done by Minerva Teichert. In this particular portrait, Esther looks unassumingly regal and possessed with a clear-eyed and quiet confidence. Sister Winkle loved that painting of Esther, and I did too. She reminded me that, along with Ruth, Esther was the only other woman who has her own book in the bible.

Sister Winkle went on to describe the importance of Esther's life. She spoke about her courage in defending and saving her people, even as she put her own life at risk. And I thought that the Lord loves strong women. And that thought made me happy. Sister Winkle told me she believed that Esther was a type of the savior, who had also saved her people. It was a singular night for me in the temple.

But it was my first trip back to the temple that touched me even more deeply in ways I hadn't anticipated. I'd been fasting and praying all day that my heart would be open to the Spirit and that my understanding might be enlarged. While it wasn't so much that I'd be hearing new things, it was that I wanted to hear old things with new ears.

Before I got to the temple, Brent called. "I have news, Susan," he said.

And I wondered: What now? He'd been full of surprising news over the past few months. And then he said, "They're sending us to New Zealand."

"New Zealand?" I asked surprised. "New Zealand?" I repeated. "When and for how long?"

"It might be for the next 4 years. But it will be at least for the next few months," he answered.

"I thought you were supposed to be in Salt Lake another eleven months," I questioned. It was going to be hard enough to have my brother take off for parts unknown. But now it was happening even earlier than I thought.

"So did we. But things have changed," he said simply.

"How soon do you go?" I asked, still stunned.

"Sometime around the middle of October. We're not sure yet."

It was then that it became clear to me why it was important for us all to be in the temple together October 5. I was grateful I'd moved forward with faith, just at the right time, as I'd been prompted to do.

I went to the temple that night with Chris, who had called our friend Jeanne to make sure she knew we were coming. So after we dressed in white, Jeanne took us to the bride's room. Among other things, Jeanne talked about the equality enjoyed by all people in the temple. She reminded us that race, color, creed, gender, and/or socioeconomic status counted for nothing in the temple. She spoke about work that women are able to do only in the temple, and I understood for the first time that the fullness of the priesthood could only be found here.

As we left the bride's room, Jeanne told me that if I had any questions following the session, she'd be happy to arrange a meeting for me with one of the members of the temple presidency. I told her that I did have some questions about family sealing ordinances, so she said she'd set up an appointment.

Jeanne then took us to the endowment room, where she seated us in the front row. As I walked into the room, I saw that Chris's husband Paul was officiating. I love Paul. His grandfather had grown up in Oakley, Idaho, and he'd known both my dad and our Haight cousins. Paul smiled and winked at me. I watched him quietly encourage me throughout the session.

I wondered if I'd remember what to do and say after such a long time. And then the words came to me, "The Lord will bring all things back to your mind, and it will be as if you had never left." And it all did come back. Just as promised. I didn't need prompting at any point. I participated fully in the session without assistance, and I was fully prepared to renew sacred covenants and obligations.

I thought as I listened to the promises we were making that the Church requires a consecrated life from its members. That was especially evident in my own family, I reflected, as I returned to Brent's earlier phone call. He and Marcia were getting ready to fly across the ocean, away from family and friends and everything that was near and dear to them, to serve the people of the Pacific area. They didn't complain or ask any questions. They were just going as they'd been called to do.

I think I understood for the first time how serious the Church is about requiring the sacrifice of both time and talents from its members. This church is not for the uncommitted or the faint of heart, I thought. And it never has been. I knew there were many faithful members living all over the world making sacrifices to serve others. And I found that impressive.

After the session ended, I got dressed. Chris drove home with Paul, and Jeanne took me to meet with President Steed. We had a warm conversation about the sealing of husbands to wives and children to parents. He answered all my questions. He was gentle and concerned, and he gave me great hope. He reminded me that while the eternal sealing of husbands to their wives could be set aside, the sealing of children to their parents never could be. Not under any circumstances.

I was worthy again of my temple blessings. Alicia and Alex would forever be mine. "Your children are still under the sealing promise," President Steed assured me. There was nothing more important to me than that in either this life or the promised life to come. I love my children more than life itself.

President Steed and I talked for some time before I rose to go. I thanked him for his time. He grasped my hand kindly and said, "Welcome home, Susan." And then as he looked at what must have been surprised eyes, he continued, "You are home now, you know." And I thought simply, someone else has looked into my heart and read my thoughts.

So this was the home I'd lost so long ago. And all this time I'd been searching for a geographic location that I could call home. No wonder I hadn't been able to find it. It wasn't for lack of trying. It was just that I was looking for home in the wrong places, when what I needed to do instead was to see my old home with new eyes.

I walked out the front doors of the temple and back out into the warm, late summer evening. I rejoiced in the beautiful fountains I saw in front of me that first pushed their waters upward and then sprayed them back down into the waiting pools below. And I knew what Sister Winkle meant when she'd described the living waters. Tears of joy streamed down my face.

# XVIII
## How My Life Had Changed

*J*was once again on a plane flying to Salt Lake City. It was October 2, 2009, and General Conference started the next day. It would be awhile before the Nielsons would all be in the same place again, I thought sadly. I was really looking forward to our time together.

And unlike General Conference last April, this time I'd be watching all the sessions, rather than viewing a few of them sporadically. This time I'd be listening to the messages as a believer, rather than as an inactive skeptic. This time I was one with the saints. It was almost impossible not to be awed at how my life had changed in six short months.

Dave, Jaci, and Mom met me at the airport. It still surprised me that Mom was a Salt Laker now. As I watched Mom walk slowly toward me, I could see even at a distance that she was much happier now than when she'd first moved to Salt Lake. Living with Dave and Jaci had strengthened her and helped make a difficult move easier.

"Is that my favorite daughter," she called out in typical fashion as she reached up for a hug. As I put my arms around her frail shoulders, we laughed. Of course it was easy to be her favorite daughter, since I was her only daughter. Dave took my bags from me and put them in the back of his car. It was an unseasonably warm, fall evening in Salt Lake. Saturday also promised to be warmer than I'd anticipated for this time of year.

I was happy that Alicia and Jenna were driving in from St George. I knew they were on the road already, so I called them from my cell phone to check in. Alicia told me they were doing fine and just a few hours out. So I sat back, relaxed, and enjoyed the short trip to Dave's house. Dave mentioned that he was sorry Alex and Karry wouldn't be coming as well. I was too.

After we pulled up in front of the house and went inside, I saw that Jaci had a tasty chocolate cake waiting for a late-night dessert. Her house was as warm and inviting as it always was, I thought, as Dave generously hefted my bags downstairs to the guest room.

We were soon sitting around the kitchen table laughing and talking, waiting for Alicia and Jenna. It wasn't much longer before they walked through the door together, arm-in-arm. I was relieved that they'd arrived safely, as I always am when my children travel. My children sometimes smile at my concern for their well being, now that they're adults. But I've found that my parental concern has not in any way diminished as my children have grown. So I gave my girls a relieved hug. Alicia and Jenna were both happy to see all of us, but my mom in particular.

Jenna has a special spot in her heart for her Grandma Lucy. I was reminded of how gently Jenna had helped her navigate in and out of the borrowed wheelchair last month, when we went with Brent and Marcia to "Music and the Spoken Word." Jenna helped her Grandma Lucy get into the chair, carefully placed her grandma's feet on the foot rests, and then insisted on being the one to push her around the grounds.

I then watched as Jenna had made an effort to match her own footsteps with the rhythm of the moving wheelchair, so it would be a smooth ride. All this while walking on a sprained and taped ankle. She was my sweetheart. So much like her Great-Grandfather Nielson, I thought, whom she regrettably had never met.

It was a late night by the time we all fell into bed. I'd be getting up early the next morning to drive to Brent and Marcia's house for breakfast in North Salt Lake. Katy and I had tickets to attend the morning session of conference together.

I arrived at Brent's house just before 7:30 a.m. Cute little Lucy was there to greet me. It was so good to see the girls again. I still missed them. I'd bought a purple "My Little Pony" for Lucy that had rainbow-colored hair and a matching purple brush. She loved it. For Claire, I bought a Winnie-the-Pooh stackable toy.

My nephew "Little" Brent and his wife Annie were also there having breakfast. As we finished breakfast, Marcia passed by me on her way into the kitchen and wrapped her arms around my shoulders from behind.

"I'm just feeling so overwhelmed with joy that you're here with us, Susan," she said. I thought that was a wonderful thing to say.

"Thank you, Marcia," I smiled up at her. "It makes me feel so good to hear you say that."

Then Katy said, "Well, I was feeling overwhelmed with joy about Susan yesterday. I just didn't say anything."

Little Brent jumped in right on Katy's heels and said, "I felt that way about Susan 2 days ago."

Not to be outdone by his children, my brother Brent offered, "I felt that way last week." And then we all laughed. I told them they'd each made me feel loved, and I appreciated them.

Then Tyler came in. I hugged him and offered a hearty congratulations on passing his bar exams. Now he was an official member of the family law firm in Twin Falls. He told me he was relieved to have passed on the first try. "There was never any doubt in my mind that you would, Tyler," I asserted truthfully. He just smiled modestly.

Tyler was staying home to watch the little girls so Katy and I could attend conference together. It was typical of him to be so considerate, I thought. "Thank you, Tyler," I smiled.

Then Katy and I said goodbye to the girls and left the house. It was a beautifully crisp fall day with brilliantly colored leaves everywhere. Katy and I got into her car and followed Brent and Marcia to the parking lot. Katy and I first parked the car and then made our way across the street to the imposing, gray conference center. There was a keen sense of anticipation in the air on the part of the almost 22,000 other faithful members who would be joining us in the conference center that morning.

There was also the usual motley assortment of protestors out front mocking the Mormons, the worst of them even resorting to waving around a pair of white garments smeared with blood on a pole. I thought as I had years ago: I get that you're telling the world what it is you're so disrespectfully and vehemently against. But what is it you're for? What do you believe instead? Wouldn't finding that out be a more productive use of your time? But I said nothing. It wouldn't change anything.

Katy and I walked past them, presented our tickets to be scanned, walked through the metal detectors, and then gave up our purses to be searched. It was sad that the Church had to implement this kind of high level security for conference, I thought, but given the crazies outside, it was obviously necessary. Katy and I found seats as close to the front as we could.

As the session began, my soul filled with both the choir's flawless singing and the incredible messages of love, guidance, and hope. I felt so blessed to be there, believing as I did now. I'd simply exceeded my threshold to contain joy. So much had happened in such a short space. So much that I would never have thought possible just 6 months ago. I only knew that it was beyond my own capacity to make this much change happen this fast.

That evening, Alicia, Jenna, Mom, Jaci, Karla, Amanda, and I went out to dinner together, while the men attended the priesthood session. I later read those talks in the Ensign. Now that I was back, I didn't want to miss a thing.

The next morning, we watched the Sunday session of conference at Dave's house. When it ended, we grabbed a quick sandwich for the road, and Mom, Dave, Jaci, my nephew Marc, his girlfriend Amanda, Alicia, Jenna, and I all piled into Dave's Tahoe for the ride downtown. It was overcast outside, and it had been raining intermittently. Today felt more like fall in Salt Lake.

As we reached the temple grounds, Dave pulled over to the curb and we all got out—all of us but Mom and Dave—to go get our seats in the conference center. When Mom finally arrived, she came and sat by me. Norm and Karla sat immediately to my right. Dave and Jaci were a little further down the row with Alicia and Jenna, my niece Amelia, and Marc and Amanda. My nephew Trent and two of his roommates sat just in back of me. Brent's family was sitting together a few rows in back of the rest of us.

A hush soon swept the hall as the red lights on the large, rolling cameras blinked and the giant monitors that were mounted on either side of the interior walls of the conference center filled with bright images of the temple grounds outside. The producer counted down on his fingers as the hall darkened, "In 5, 4, 3, 2, 1" And then on cue, the choir raised their voices to sing. As I looked around at the masses of Mormons flanking me, it was with the sense that I was again an integral part of this large community of faith.

A few of the speakers' messages resonated with me very personally that Sunday afternoon. One of them was Elder Dale Renlund's talk on "Preserving the Mighty Change of Heart." After all I'd been through, his message was particularly poignant for me. As a former heart surgeon, Elder Renlund spoke knowingly about how a patient's own body will reject a brand new life-saving heart as foreign and will begin to attack it. Then he drew the parallel between a new physical heart and a new spiritual heart. He cautioned that even greater care must be taken with a spiritually changed heart. He counseled his listeners to read scriptures, pray, seek the constant companionship of the Holy Ghost, and help and serve others.

As I listened to his words, I knew he was right. I knew that I could not afford to be casual with my newly-changed heart. I understood better than many in that room how easy it was veer off track and disappear into the mist. Not for me. Not ever again.

Time sped quickly by for me as I listened to the remainder of the speakers. President Monson eventually closed the conference by advising all of us to "do good continually." He talked about how we are all in this together and asked that God would give us the strength to play our part well. My eyes again filled with tears. I wanted to again play my part well. Whatever that part might turn out to be.

After the meeting ended, Marcia found me, hugged me, and whispered in my ear that she was so glad I'd been there with the family. I sobbed into her shoulder as I thought about how close I'd come to not being there with them that day. If I hadn't listened to the whisperings of the Spirit and come back to the Church when I did, I might have missed it all. I was so thankful I hadn't.

# XXIX

## The Hearts of the Children

*"One thing have I desired of the Lord . . .
that I may dwell in the house of the Lord all the days
of my life, to behold the beauty of the Lord,
and to enquire in his temple."—Psalm 27:4*

*D*ave, Jaci, Mom and I got up early Monday morning to drive downtown to the Salt Lake temple. My mom had been waiting for this day forever. My recommend was still new to me, and I didn't take it for granted when the gentle man behind the desk scanned it, handed it back to me, and with a smile said, "Welcome to the temple."

While I'd been on the outside of the Salt Lake temple many times over the past 15 years, it had been a long time since I'd been inside its walls. I'd forgotten how large and historic this beautiful building really is, I thought, as I admired its furnishings. I remembered that it was here that I'd taken out my own endowments, here that I was married, and here that both my babies had been sealed to me. This was also the only temple I'd been in with my dad.

I made my way quickly downstairs to the baptistery. One of the workers there handed me a white jumpsuit and a large white towel. My brothers had decided that just one of us would go down into the waters of baptism on behalf of the female family names we were taking through, and just one of us would go into the water for the male names. Little Brent and I were the fortunate two.

I walked across the white marble floors of the baptistery to the large baptismal font that sits on the back of the 12 life-sized cast iron oxen below. Dave waded first into the shallow water and then extended his hand to help me down the stairs. Norm sat at the top of the steps, waiting to perform the confirmations. Mom sat up top in a chair off to the side, observing the proceedings closely, and Brent and Tyler sat at a small table on the south side as witnesses. Marcia and Jaci, and my nieces Emily, Katy, and Annie stood around the railing of the font watching with big smiles on their faces. The temple is for families, I thought. And I was grateful to be here with so many of mine.

As Dave raised his arm to the square, he repeated the words of the ordinance, and then laid me under the water. I tried to concentrate on each name individually. I tried to think about how each one of them might be feeling to be baptized members of their family's church. I pictured joy and rejoicing on the other side of the veil. I knew my own face was beaming, because I had to keep reminding myself to stop smiling and just hold my breath as I went under the water again

Then Norm conferred the Gift of the Holy Ghost. It's impossible to write even a small part of what I felt as we completed these ordinances. Marcia later wrote in an email, "I don't know who was in charge of helping from behind the veil on getting this day to happen, but it must have been an all out crack squad team of interventionists." I suspected that she was right.

After we completed the initiatory work, we put on our white dresses and met the men in the large temple chapel. We were flanked by two large murals painted by artist Harris Wiberg, one of the Mount of Olives and one of Christ's ascension into heaven. We sat together as a family and appreciated the time to just be still.

We went next to the creation room and then to the lovely garden room, whose walls and ceilings are filled with beautiful oil paintings of flowers, birds, and brooks of water. I enjoyed the live session as the plan of God unfolded before us. When we entered the final ordinance room, I remembered being there more than 30 years ago, when I'd received my own endowments.

It had been a unique and unusual experience for me that day, and I had felt more than a little overwhelmed—until I walked into this room and saw my dad sitting along a bench in the front of the room, next to the veil. He smiled at me, and I relaxed. He made everything all right. I felt safe and cared for.

I looked to the spot where Dad had sat before, and I felt him there with me again today. And why wouldn't he be here? For the first time in 15 years, there were no empty chairs. Dad wouldn't have missed this day, I thought, as we all stood together in prayer. It was an emotional moment for all of us.

We went next to the Celestial room. We stayed there awhile hugging and speaking in whispered voices. This has got to be one of the most beautiful rooms anywhere in the world, I thought looking around me at its curved couches, its arched doorways, and old lighted chandeliers. It's a place of such serenity and peace. Marcia wrote later, "How wonderful to see Susan there with us. It was incredible actually." I thought it was incredible too. And I knew this was the day the Lord intended for us to be the temple together, before Brent and Marcia left for New Zealand for their new assignment with the Church. There would never again be another day like today.

We went next into one of the sealing rooms off the Celestial room. We sat in padded chairs facing the plush altar, where we would soon kneel in sacred ordinances. Brent performed all the sealing work. The rest of us took turns representing our ancestors as Brent sealed husbands to wives and children to parents for eternity. This is exactly what the Church is all about, I thought. "And he shall turn the heart of the fathers to the children, and the heart of the children to their fathers" Malachi 4:6

We spoke openly about the day's experiences. We talked about my dad and how much we'd all felt him there with us in the temple. It was a special and sacred experience, and one that I will never forget. We left the temple reluctantly and went to get dressed into our street clothes.

We walked outside into the fall sunshine, and Annie put her camera on a tripod, set the timer, and took a picture of all of us out there on the green lawns of the temple grounds. My mom looked radiant in her blue dress, white hair, and face glowing. It was an indescribable day for all of us.

Marcia later wrote to my nephew Dave: "I never want to forget how happy I feel to have Susan back in the spiritual part of our lives. She is incredible, David. She looks even more beautiful with the sweetness of the gospel in her eyes. We are having a wonderful time talking more openly about the Church and anticipating even better things to come."

And I thought: "Behold, he changed their hearts; yea he awakened them out of a deep sleep, and they awoke unto God." Alma 5:7

# Part 5

# WITH THE VOICE OF THANKSGIVING

*That I may publish with the voice of Thanksgiving;*
*and tell of all thy wondrous works.*

—PSALM 26:7

# XXX

## Out With the Missionaries

*A*s I continued my journey home, I found myself anxious to begin giving back to others in return for what others had done for me. I got my first opportunity a few weeks after conference, when Elder Henderson and Elder Hansen, the missionaries assigned to our ward, asked me to go on "splits" with them to help teach a new member lesson to the Carmichaels. Mike and Diane Carmichael lived in my ward, and they had just joined the Church. I'd first met Diane on the tennis courts. I'd met Mike later at our empty nesters group. They were a great couple.

I was generally eager to help the elders. But I'd only been back in the Church for not quite 6 months. And I'd never done anything remotely similar to going out to teach with the missionaries. Even when I was at my most active. So I was a little nervous about the whole idea. Elder Henderson assured me that I'd do fine, so I agreed to go.

After one of Diane's signature dinners of spaghetti and homemade meat balls, we all settled in on her family room couches with the elders' favorite dessert: peach tart with vanilla ice cream. Diane had also made Elder Henderson a beautiful charcoal scarf for him to wear when he rode his bike out in the cold Sacramento nights. I teased the elders that I hadn't realized just how good they had it out here in the Sacramento mission. I told them I was pretty sure that my two missionary nephews, one in Japan and the other in Latvia, weren't quite as fortunate.

The elders had assigned me to talk about how much God loves us. I shared my testimony about how God is in the details of each one of our lives. I told the Carmichaels a little bit about what had brought me back to the Church and how happy coming back had made me. Then I spoke about Christ's purpose for coming to earth and the blessings of the atonement. Elder Henderson kindly held up his flip chart and pointed to the requisite pictures for me when I got stuck, reminding me what to say next.

Then the elders spoke about the apostasy and the restoration. And then I talked about the Book of Mormon. Me. I was actually teaching new members about the Book of Mormon. I heard myself providing reasons why the Lord had selected a simple farm boy to bring forth a "marvelous work and a wonder." I talked about how Joseph Smith had translated the plates in 60 days without going back and editing what he'd already translated. I'd found that particularly impressive. I spoke about why the amazing story about plates and angels was true.

I was blessed far more that night than the Carmichaels were. When we left, Elder Henderson told me that I'd done an "awesome job," my first night as a missionary. I was happy to think that might be true. And I found it simply incredible to sit in people's homes and see firsthand how the Church transforms their lives for the better. I marveled again at how coming back to the Church had made such positive changes in my own.

Almost one year to the day later, I was privileged to go with the Carmichael's through the Sacramento temple, where they had their marriage sealed for eternity. Almost everyone in the Sacramento mission had rejoiced over the Carmichael's joining the Church. President Jardine had extended Elder Hansen's mission a few days so he could be there to go through the temple with the Carmichaels. He'd also let Elder Henderson, who'd been out just over a year now, leave his area for the evening so he could join us in the temple too. I was so happy to see both of those elders again! I couldn't hug them, so I settled for pumping their hands warmly and smiling a lot.

Mike and Diane had asked Merrill Hales to perform their sealing. Merrill's wife Carolee was there too, along with many of the empty nesters. Merrill gave the Carmichaels wonderful counsel as he pronounced the sealing. Mike and Diane both had tears in their eyes as they knelt across the altar from each other. They were so happy—and a bit overwhelmed, I'd say. But happy.

Also joining us that day in the temple were Diane's cousins from Arizona. She'd never met them before. Diane didn't even know she had cousins in Arizona. Let alone cousins who were members of the Church. She thought she was the only member in her family—until she started doing her genealogy. Then she found family she didn't even know she had. Her newly found cousins had flown in to go through the temple with Mike and Diane. It was an incredible experience for all of us.

I thought again about how much the Church changes people's lives when I met a woman in my stake who'd been converted to the Church as a teenager in Japan. She told me simply that she was convinced by the Joseph Smith story, even though she wasn't a Christian. Her family was Buddhist. But her heart was touched, the whole incredible Book of Mormon story made sense to her, and she was converted.

Her parents finally gave their permission for her to be baptized a few years later. After she finished school, she moved to the United States. She is now married and the mother of her own teenage daughters. Her life was never the same after she joined the Church. But whose is? I thought.

A few months later, I met a senior missionary couple in Hong Kong who were friends of my cousins Nancy and John. Brother Smith had been a professor at BYU with John. The Smiths were now serving in Asia. When I met Sister Smith, she told us she'd just spent her 77th birthday riding elephants in Thailand. She told us her grandchildren were very proud of her. And I thought, now that's how I'd like to spend my 77th birthday!

It seemed to me then that the purpose of missionary work is to effect the transformation of both the receiver and the transmitter of the message. And I was grateful for the opportunity to have had a small taste of the missionary experience.

# XXXI
## Off the Ground

*I* was in downtown Sacramento having lunch with one of my colleagues. In my excitement over the many humanitarian services I was now aware that the Church provided, I was telling her about our church's wheelchair program. Maybe it was because I'd recently met Sister Eubanks, the director of The Wheelchair Initiative for the Humanitarian Services for the Church. Or perhaps it was because I was prompted to tell my colleague and friend about our wheelchair program. Or perhaps it was a combination of both.

My friend is Hmong. When she was very young, her family escaped the Viet Cong by crossing the Mei Kong Delta from Laos into Thailand. Her father had been a freedom fighter for the United States, until South Vietnam fell to the North. Her family had left Laos under gunfire, first giving some of their money to their Thai rescuers, and then having the rest of it taken from them. They lived in refugee camps until some of their family members, who had already left Laos and settled in Minnesota, brought them to live in the United States.

My friend has an uncle and cousins who are still living in Laos. They live in the mountains in a remote village, and they are very poor. My friend's cousin needed a wheelchair. Simply put, he wanted to get off the ground.

My friend's eyes widened as I described my church's wheelchair program. "Do you think your church could help my family in Laos?" she asked me hopefully. And then she told me all about her cousin, Thao Toe.

"I don't see why not," I replied.

My friend is not a member of our church, which was of no consequence to anyone at all in terms of getting a wheelchair for her cousin.

My friend is, in fact, a deeply religious Buddhist, who believes that everything happens for a reason. She didn't think our conversation that day was a coincidence, and neither did I. Nor did anyone else who was connected with the events that followed.

I contacted Brent and asked him if he'd be willing to submit a request to Sister Eubanks, and he contacted her right away. She asked him to tell me to send her the necessary information, along with the address of my friend's cousin in Vientiane, Laos, which I did in a letter. I told Sister Eubanks that anything she could do would be appreciated. She then put an amazing chain of events in motion.

She sent my letter first to the Asia Area Welfare office in Hong Kong. Someone there forwarded it to the country director in Laos, who then gave the letter to a senior missionary couple serving in Laos, Elder and Sister Riser. They were managing the wheelchair project in Laos. When the Risers received the letter, they were getting ready to sign an agreement on behalf of the Church with the Association for Aid and Relief-Japan (AAR) and the National Rehabilitation Center of Laos (NRC).

Once the agreement was signed, the Risers asked the AAR to assess Thao Toe's needs. So the AAR scheduled a trip to see him. When the assessment was completed, the AAR team made the decision that Thao Toe would benefit most of all from a tricycle kind of device. Because he couldn't walk, he had developed a very strong upper body. The AAR reported to the Risers that they would build the right kind of device for Thao Toe.

It would take about a month to build the custom device, and it would be ready to deliver the first part of April. Elder Riser would later describe it as "an incredible chain of events that testifies of our Heavenly Father's love for his children—each and every one—all over the world."

When I told my friend that the wheelchair was being built for her cousin, she couldn't believe it. "It's such a small world in your church," she said. And I had to agree. I couldn't quite believe it either. My friend told me she was very grateful for the help from our church. Elder Riser later sent us both pictures of her family in Laos.

When the tricycle (TRI) was ready to be delivered, the Risers decided to go along. What follows is the partial text of an email that Elder Riser later sent to Sister Eubanks, Brent, and me.

"We had the privilege of going with the members of the AAR team to deliver the tricycle. The experience is one of the highlights of our mission. Ban Nam Pong is a remote village accessed by a long, steep, and very bumpy road. We've been on a lot of bumpy roads in the mountains of Utah, but this was the king of long, bumpy roads. Our group was in two different cars: AAR was in a Prado with the TRI on top. [The rest of us] followed in President Khamphee's van.

We observed the family as we parked the cars and as they saw the TRI. They knew we were coming, and they were waiting. Thao Toe saw the device on top of the vehicle and [knew] immediately that it was for him. His smile was HUGE. None of us was prepared to see him move across the yard so fast. His strong arms literally propelled him over the hard-packed dirt. He was into the device as soon as it was rolled into the yard.

We waited for help translating (the family speaks Hmong—we had only Lao and English speakers—) so someone ran to get the village chief who knows Lao and Hmong. We showed Thao Toe the bell on the handle bars and watched him glow. It made us smile too. The AAR team instructed [him] and his family in the use of the TRI and let [him] practice in the road.

We took a lot of pictures, soaked in being there, etched the scene in our memories, and then said good-bye to our new forever friends. We [were] awed with the scope of the Humanitarian Services of the Church, the resources that are available to help the people of the world, and that the system really works."

I was amazed at Elder Riser's letter. And I knew he was right when he said that our Heavenly Father knows his children and is concerned about each one. On that day in April, the Lord was in the details of a 19-year old Hmong boy's life in an isolated village in Laos. For my part, I was just happy to participate in a small piece of that experience. Mostly, I was grateful for all the caring people in this chain of events who had made it all possible. I was astonished at the scope of the Church's resources to do good works in the world.

I don't always know when the Lord is in the details of my own life, the lives of my children, or the lives of others like Thao Toe. But I think I might understand the how. The Lord was in the details of Thao Toe's life that day because others listened to and acted on spiritual promptings. My life and the lives of others are blessed when we are engaged in God's work.

I found myself wishing that I could just "do good continually." On some particularly long work days of my own, I still struggled to be "in, but not of the world." I struggled to hone my compassion. And some days just to sustain my faith.

But I always knew the end goal. I occasionally caught glimpses of what I still needed to become. And I tried to look daily for ways to both give thanks and to give back to others.

# XXXII

## A New Year

*I*'d just spent my first Christmas as a believer in a long time. The season had been so much sweeter this year, I thought, looking at the nativity scene still sitting on top of my black piano. I saw the crèche now not as a representation of someone else's belief, but as a symbol of my own.

The missionaries had come over before Christmas to help me put up my tree and my outside lights. I took the three of them out to dinner and offered to call each of their moms to say hello from El Dorado Hills and tell them what generous sons they had. Elder Henderson's mother in particular cried and was so happy to hear about her boy.

I also went to our ward Christmas party this year. And to a Christmas concert at the Mormon Center. Then on December 18, I flew to Orange County to spend the day at Disneyland with Alex and Karry, Brent and Annie, and their little boys.

Brent and Annie were very patient with me when I indulged a request from Will for a Mickey Mouse ice cream sandwich, which I bought him on the way to our picnic lunch. Will and I came to the table proudly holding aloft ice cream sandwiches for him and his brothers. So the boys ate dessert first. Sandwiches second.

Alex accused me of being a shameless aunt who bribed her little nephews. He was right, of course. But I happily accepted this fact about myself and had no intent whatsoever to change. As a great-aunt/grandma, I was no longer concerned about such things. "Just wait until you and Karry have children," I warned him. "You'll be in such trouble." He groaned and knew I was right.

We went on the Jungle Cruise ride after lunch. I was accompanied by little Jake. He'd been on this ride recently and knew all about the new snapping piranhas. When I picked him up, he took my face in both of his small hands and looking me squarely in my eyes said solemnly, "I'll protect you, Susan. And then you can protect me."

I looked at him seriously, holding back a smile, and nodded, "You got it, Jake."

True to his word, he spent the entire ride holding my hand and watching anxiously over the side of the boat, waiting for the piranhas to strike. When they finally surfaced at the end of the ride, I had to agree with him that they were pretty scary looking things. And there were a lot of them. We had a fun day together in the Magic Kingdom.

Just before Christmas, Mom, Alicia, and Jenna had flown in to Sacramento to spend Christmas with me. It was 4 generations of just us girls. We talked and laughed and ate too much. We stayed up late and watched movies together in our fuzzy bunnies. We slept in every morning. It was pretty much just one giant slumber party.

On Christmas morning, we called Alex and Karry on Skype and opened presents together. Alex and Karry were in the throes of intense wedding preparations. They were going to be married in March. Alex and Karry's wedding was the single event I was most looking forward to in 2010.

After we signed off from talking with Alex and Karry, we Skyped with Brent and Marcia in New Zealand. Brent carried his laptop around their townhome in Auckland, giving us an on-screen tour of all the rooms with his web cam. He even took his computer out on the balcony and tried to show us their view of the ocean, but it was so bright outside, we couldn't really see the water.

The other event I was looking most forward to in the upcoming year was my trip to New Zealand in February. I wanted to see where Brent and Marcia lived. I wanted to see what they did on a daily basis, because I didn't really know. I wanted to be able to picture them in their new lives when I thought about them. When Katy heard I was going, she wanted to come along and bring the girls. So we were all going to New Zealand together in a few months.

By the time New Year's Eve rolled around, Alicia and Jenna had gone back to Utah. So Mom and I went out to dinner and a movie without them. We missed our girls. Mom went to bed about 11, so I stayed up and rang in the New Year by myself, watching the ball drop in Times Square on TV.

I thought about how much I'd enjoyed New Year's Eve last year in Sydney watching the fireworks explode over the water. And I found myself feeling just a little bit lonely and a little bit wistful about parts of my life I'd given up when I returned to the Church.

This can't be good, I thought. So I picked up the January Ensign and found an article Elder Holland had written titled, "The Best Is Yet to Be." What a hopeful title, I said aloud, and what a perfect article for me to read just as the New Year begins.

Elder Holland counseled, "Look ahead and remember that faith is always pointed toward the future." And then he cautioned, "Remember Lot's wife." He offered a new slant on the old biblical story. He said he believed that Lot's wife's problem wasn't just that she looked back on Sodom and Gomorrah. But that she looked back longingly. She looked back and wanted to *go* back. She missed what Sodom and Gomorrah had offered her. Then Elder Holland quoted Neal A. Maxwell: "Such people know that they should have their primary residence in Zion, but they still hope to keep a summer cottage in Babylon."

Elder Holland went on to advise, "The past is to be learned from, but not lived in . . . We look back to claim the embers, not the ashes." Good advice for me. I needed to be "faith forward" and not looking back on my old life out of the Church. I didn't want to look back. And I didn't want to look back longingly. Then Elder Holland said, "Lot's wife doubted the Lord's ability to give her something better than she already had." That particular statement resonated with me.

I believed that the Lord had changed my life in incredible ways. Certainly I had something much better now than what I had before. I was happy and I was at peace. There was no point in looking back. Ever.

Elder Holland ended his article by saying, "Live to see the miracles of repentance and forgiveness, of trust and divine love that will transform your life today, tomorrow, and forever." And I reminded myself that it wasn't just about change. It was about transformation.

But I still found that maintaining my change of heart was more difficult at some times than others. My change was harder to sustain when I was back in familiar situations with people who encouraged old habits. I made a mental note to avoid these kinds of business settings when possible and to be fully prepared with my response when they were absolutely unavoidable. The next time, I was ready. The time after that, it wasn't even an issue. Now I don't even think about it at all. And neither does anyone else.

I had the good sense to call my brother Dave later that week. We talked for over an hour. We connected. He encouraged me. I felt good. I was at peace again. But how best to keep this spirit of light and peace with me always?

I reminded myself that maintaining change takes both time and ongoing effort. I realized that putting myself in supportive environments with supportive people would help me sustain the change that had been so important to me to make. I'd been out of the Church for 14 years. I'd been back only 8 months. Be patient, I reminded myself.

I'd felt the mighty change of heart. But I found that I still had to work to sustain it. Similar to everyone else. The important thing was to continue to move forward until my new way of being in the world became more comfortable than the old one. I eventually got there a few months later. Just about the time I hit my year mark back in the Church.

# XXXIII

## At Home with the Kiwis

By February, Katy and the girls and I were in the Los Angeles airport getting ready to board our flight for New Zealand. Lucy was literally hopping on one foot across the floor with excitement about flying on such a big plane to see her grandparents. She had no idea how long it was going to take us to get there.

After flying all night and losing a day, we landed in Auckland about 5:30 Saturday morning. We tumbled wearily off the plane, claimed our luggage, and made our way through customs. Brent and Marcia were waiting for us on the other side. As soon as we saw them, Lucy and Claire ran squealing into their arms. Then it was Katy's turn. And then it was mine. We were all happy to see each other. Brent and Marcia hadn't seen anyone in their family for 4 months. Christmas had been an especially quiet time for them, so I was especially glad we were here now.

We drove to Brent and Marcia's townhome in Takapuna Beach, which is a suburb of Auckland. It was in an amazing location right on the water. And it was within walking distance of the Pacific Area offices where Brent worked. After dropping our bags in our rooms, Katy and I walked straight out onto the back deck to find a stunning 180 degree view of the blue-green ocean, white sail boats tacking across the water, and the looming dormant volcano Rangitoto off in the distance in front of us.

Brent told us that Rangitoto meant "Blood Sky" in Maori. I for one was hoping never to see first hand why the Maoris had dubbed this particular volcano Rangitoto. But as the days passed, I loved watching what I called the many faces of Rangitoto, which started first with the brilliant orange of the early morning sky, moved through blue-white afternoons, and culminated in the ink-black night sky, accented by a bright moon that rose behind the cone of the volcano.

Katy, the girls, and I did our best to stay up all day the first day we were there. After unpacking, we all had breakfast at a small open air sidewalk café and then went to a little market to shop. On the way home, I found myself falling asleep sitting up in the van. By 7:00 that night, I couldn't take it any more. I went straight to bed and slept with the windows wide open and the fan running at full speed. It was a deliciously warm, February night. Once my head hit the pillow, I didn't move a muscle or hear another thing until 6 the next morning. I awoke refreshed with no jet lag.

When everyone else was up, we packed small overnight bags for our trip to Hamilton after church. Brent and Marcia had been asked to speak at a tri-stake institute devotional that night. They were off on Monday, as they are every Monday, so while we were in the Hamilton area, we planned to spend Monday in Rotorua.

As we left Takapuna Beach, we had to take back streets to avoid the growing crowds. The main streets were blocked off for the Iron Man Triathlon. Before leaving for church, we had watched from the outside deck as hordes of swimmers in yellow caps ran madly across the beach and plunged into the ocean, marking the beginning of the swimming portion of the triathlon. For some of them, the goal was to win. For others it was simply to be able to finish what they had started.

After church ended, we drove several hours north to Hamilton. We would be spending that night at the Quantum Motor Lodge, which turned out to be a townhome arrangement with a hot tub out on the back deck. The next morning's breakfast was included, and we were given cold bottles of fresh milk upon check in. I liked that particular custom.

That night, Katy stayed at the motel with two very tired little girls, and I went with Brent and Marcia to Muir Park Chapel. When I looked at the program, I saw that the theme for the devotional was "Finishers Wanted." I remembered the triathlon participants back in Auckland, who were in a race of another kind, and I immediately felt sad that I'd made my own very wide and very long spiritual detour. I consoled myself with the promise that now that I was back in the race, I was determined once again to be a finisher.

One of the speakers talked about spiritual shelter and quoted from Jacob: "It is the word that healeth the wounded soul." Then he said that God never intended for us to be alone and that we each had a community of faith to support us. As I listened, I was ever so glad I'd found my way back to my community of faith. I was so much happier having a strong religious identity and good people to share it with.

Brent's talk was on the revelatory process and the importance of taking time to just sit and ponder, read the scriptures, and pray. To me, that sounded as if it would be a welcome break from living in a world where I was almost always wirelessly connected to someone or something that I typically could neither see nor touch.

Brent told about when he and Marcia had first come to New Zealand. He described the challenges of driving in the roundabouts. Not being used to driving on the left-hand side of the road, Brent talked about the number of times they'd been stuck in the roundabouts, trying to decide which way to go. There was lots of laughter when Brent talked about the difficulty in navigating the round abouts. He then drew the parallel about the importance of not getting stuck in spiritual round abouts. Having been stuck there myself for such a long time, I knew precisely what he meant.

Brent then said that there were 3 unbreakable appointments in life: daily prayer, daily scripture study, and daily time spent with family. As he concluded his talk, he and Marcia took any and all questions from the audience. Marcia was honest and direct. Brent was gentle and eloquent. Together, they made a great team.

Brent ended the meeting with a reference to D&C 123: "Do your best cheerfully and leave the rest to the Lord." It was good advice. I found that there were some questions for which I simply had the wrong answers. There were other questions that just could not be answered at all. And there were still other questions that were simply irrelevant. Given all that ambiguity, why not just stay in a worthwhile race and be a finisher? I asked myself.

I spent the next few days enjoying Maori arts and crafts or just shopping and walking on the beach. Then I flew with Marcia to Queenstown to spend a little time on South Island, which was even more beautiful than North Island, if that were possible.

We spent a wonderful couple of days together looking at the gorgeous scenery, frisky dolphins, and slick little fur seals. We took a boat trip down Milford Sound and were astounded by the majesty of Mitre Peak. I thought the fjords were amazing, as I saw those sheer cliffs rise straight up out of the water. For the trip back to Queenstown from Milford Sound, Marcia and I opted to board a small six-seater plane, dipping our way through the fjords and then over the tops of the Southern Alps back to Queenstown. It was one of the highlights of my trip.

A few days later, after Marcia and I got back from South Island, Katy and I walked over to the area offices, while Marcia stayed home to play with the little girls. It was such a lovely summer morning—I had to keep reminding myself that it was still winter in my part of the world. Katy and I got to the offices a few minutes early and settled into some seats close to the front. We'd come over this particular morning because Brent was delivering a devotional to the Church employees.

Brent's talk was about prayer, which, in the beginning, seemed to be an innocuous enough topic. He began by saying that God is our father and wants us to communicate with him. Ok. I understood that. Then Brent referenced part of the Bible Dictionary's definition of prayer. How is it that I'd never read this definition in the Bible Dictionary? I thought as he continued. And this is where things took a twist—at least in my mind. Part of the definition read, "The object of prayer is not to change the will of God, but to secure for ourselves and for others blessings that God is already willing to grant."

That way of looking at the purpose of prayer changed things for me, both about how I'd been praying and how I perhaps should be praying. It also changed what I might expect to get from prayer. Aligning my will with the will of God meant that I couldn't just pray for every good thing that I wanted to come into my life or the lives of my children and expect life to happen just as I thought it should. It was also impossible that "God's will" meant that I would always be physically protected from the angry, thoughtless, or sometimes evil deeds of others. Even God could not tamper with the law of agency. I knew myself well enough to know that I had never made room in my prayers for the possibility of tragedies large or small, natural or otherwise, to strike me or anyone I loved. But they had anyway. Both me and *everybody* else in some form or another. I'd lived long enough to see that.

Things had gone awry in my life. I'd suffered. I'd felt pain. I'd cried foul. This wasn't how my life was supposed to turn out, I'd lamented. But lamenting what I could not change, changed nothing. It was simply a waste of precious time.

As I looked back from my current vantage point, I could see that my challenges had made me resilient; that my pain had made me more compassionate; that my doubts had sown seeds of faith. And if it were true that I could only take with me what I'd become in this life, then maybe God had answered my prayers in ways that I hadn't realized: Maybe he'd given me the time and space to grow.

I had to learn to accept the good with the bad and find out what God had in mind for me, and not what I had in mind for me. I decided that while God could not always provide for my physical protection, he would always provide for my spiritual protection, unless I got in my own way. God would always be there to heal my heart, if I would reach out and ask in faith.

It all seemed so simple now that I thought about it. I'd made it unnecessarily complex. And along the way, I'd forgotten to count my blessings, naming them "one by one." I'd focused on the lack in my life, not the abundance, and I'd made myself poorer in the process. Would I go back even now and choose my trials? No. But would I change the person overcoming those challenges had helped me become? Never.

Brent finished his talk, and everyone filed out. Katy and I went up to Brent's office, and I asked him to give me a blessing. Many of the words he spoke in that blessing were of particular importance to me. A few of the words he said to me were these:

"The Lord knows you by name. There has been great rejoicing on both sides of the veil over your return to the gospel. Your testimony will continue to grow and increase. When you have doubts, remember how the Lord spoke to your mind. Use the temple as a place of solace and learning. Listen for both what is spoken and unspoken.

Your family loves you. We have always loved you. Be close to your brothers and mother and to your nieces and nephews. Know that you are not alone: We stand on your right hand and your left hand to help you in any way that we can. Go forward with faith and the knowledge that the Lord loves you. Make your will one with his."

I was very grateful for Brent's blessing, and for the support of a loving family that I had always had, in or out of the Church. And then I thought, there it is again—the need to make my will one with God's will. And I understood that while I might fill my prayers with timetables, God did not necessarily share those timetables with me. It would be a wonderful way for me to learn patience, I reasoned, which I have never had in rich supply.

I had been blessed in so many ways during my two weeks here in New Zealand. I knew that all of God's blessings were open to all his children, which is the only way it really can be or should be. And that made me happy.

The next morning, I packed. My two weeks in New Zealand had flown by far too quickly. I spent the last day kayaking with Katy, sitting in the hot tub with Marcia and the little girls, and just walking on the beach, looking at Rangitoto off in the distance. I had come to love the sight of that dormant volcano. It had been a fantastic and life-altering two weeks for me, but it was time to go home now. My son's wedding was only 3 weeks away.

# XXXIV

## The Last Dance

*B*efore I knew it, it was Alex and Karry's wedding week. It had been an emotional few months for me as I prepared for yet another transition in Alex's life and in mine too. My baby was getting married, and I found that I wasn't really as ready as I'd thought. The reality was that I was no longer the most important woman in his life, as I had been ever since that squirmy little baby boy first wormed his way into my life, mind, and heart.

Alex had been a joy from the very beginning. He'd always embraced life with energy, enthusiasm, and an open heart. His excitement and trust were palpable. When he was a baby, I rocked him to sleep; when he was a toddler, I tucked him in at night; and when he decided he was too old for tucks, we renamed our nightly ritual "lay bys." Soon even the "lay bys" got too babyish, and we began calling them chats. Eventually, we simply went out to dinner to "talk about our feelings."

As Alex got into high school, we argued about how many shop classes were too many or how old too old was for a curfew. There were days when I embarrassed him, and there were times when he challenged me. But whether he was 5 or 25, when he came through the door with his big "Hi Mom" and a grin that started in his wide eyes and traveled across his warm, gentle face, my mother's heart always melted in my chest.

And now I was about to be replaced by the new woman in his life—really this is how I wanted it to be. I loved Karry, and I knew they'd be good together.

It was now only two days until their wedding. As I packed my bags to fly to Orange County, my sense of loss was growing. As I boarded the plane, I chose a seat by the window for the flight out, so I could see the outline of the ocean from the air, which never failed to delight me.

I landed, found my big, black bag with the broken zipper, and made my way to the rental car booth. The earnest gum cracker behind the counter told me there was a 45-minute wait for cars, then asked me if I was alone. Since we were the only two in the office, I assured her that I was. She told me that I could have a two-door Camero with limited trunk space, if I didn't want to wait, which I didn't.

My only thought as I climbed into the fire-engine red Camero was that I hoped I wouldn't get pulled over on the freeway. But as I pulled out onto the open highway and into the warm, California sunshine, I found myself sailing through green hills and loving the way the car handled under my touch. Maybe this wasn't such a bad thing after all.

The next day was the wedding rehearsal dinner. We piled into multiple cars to make our way to the rehearsal dinner. My brother Dave and nephew Marc came with me in the Camero. We drove down the hill from San Clemente and onto Pacific Coast Highway. I was so distracted, I almost passed Salt Creek Grille. I made a sharp right up Crown Valley and pulled into the parking lot. I was happy to hand the car off to the valet.

After I walked up the steps to the restaurant, I passed the blazing open fire pits surrounded by the comfortable, old outside couches and thought of nights Alex and I had gone there for dinner. I found myself laughing and sharing a "bruschetta" story with my brothers.

As we walked through the restaurant to the Monarch Room, I heard Alex call, "Mom! Looks who's here!" I turned and walked back to find Alex chatting with Bridgette, his old boss at the Mail Room, and her family. It all felt so warm and familiar.

Dinner passed without incident. I decided to begin the toasting just before dessert was served. I approached the microphone, my story about Karry and how she was there for Alex when he had his emergency appendectomy fixed firmly in my mind. More toasts from family and friends, and the night ended as suddenly as it began.

After dinner ended, we drove back to our hotel in San Clemente. Mom, Alicia, Jenna, and I were sharing a room. Mom and I took the two beds. Alicia and Jenna slept on the pull-out couches. I was in and out of the bathroom most of the night with a queasy stomach. "What's wrong, Mom?" Alicia asked me sleepily after the third trip.

"I don't know," I answered her. "Must have been something I ate."

Alicia smiled. "I don't think that's it, Mom."

"What do you think it is, then?" I asked surprised.

"You're nervous about the wedding, Mom. It's a big change in your life to have your baby get married."

"Do you seriously think that's it? I never get so nervous that I get sick," I responded.

"Tonight you do," Alicia said. "And I get it, Mom. It's a big change for me too."

"It is?" I asked, unfortunately not understanding what she meant.

"Yes, Mom. I'm not your only daughter anymore. Now you have two daughters."

Feeling both clueless and insensitive, I hugged her. "Not to worry, sweetheart. You'll always be my number one girl." It seemed that I'd been thinking about no one but me. What a surprise.

Finally the wedding day arrived. I watched my tall and handsome Alex stand in his carefully fitted tux across from his beautiful and hopeful Kare-Bear. He recited his vows with tears of love running down his face. Never had I seen my son so moved, or so vulnerable, standing there under the cubed arbor his dad had so lovingly and painstakingly constructed for him.

My brother Dave officiated at the wedding. As the wedding party and guests sat looking out over the shiny waters of the Pacific, Dave counseled Alex and Karry to pray both with and for each other every night. He advised them that from this day on they were bound to each other and none else. He told them there was no room in their relationship for a third party—not a parent, and not a friend. They were each other's best friends now, to love and to cherish; to have and to hold; from this day forward.

I looked over at Karry's dad Pete and wondered if he were as unprepared to lose his little girl as I was to lose my little boy. And I decided he probably was.

Karry said her vows. She promised to love and protect the heart of my son, and I was grateful for her words. And then I listened as Dave pronounced Alex and Karry husband and wife. They looked so happy as they kissed each other.

Later that night at the wedding reception, Alex and I danced our last mother/son dance together to the strains of Natalie Cole singing, "Unforgettable." Which it was. And he was.

As we returned to our chairs, I looked around the room to find myself surrounded by family and friends. I was encased in their warmth. I had a community of faith both here and waiting for me back home. My life had changed in ways that I found both sweet and bittersweet.

As I looked at the happy couple sitting across the room, I thought of the words to one of my favorite Robert Browning poems, "Come grow old with me, the best is yet to be." And I smiled, because I believed it was true. And I did not doubt God's ability to make all of our lives even better. And for that, I was grateful.

# XXXV

## Just Like My Mom

It was the day after Thanksgiving. After a lazy, sleep in kind of a morning, Alicia, Jenna, and I rode up to the little town of Springdale, Utah, which sits at the entrance to the massive red and white-rock cliffs of Zion's National Park. The sky was a stellar blue as we wound our way up to the mouth of the canyon. I sat comfortably stretched out in the back seat of Alicia's car, and Jenna sat up front, where she could control the radio.

"How's the car working for you, Alicia?" I asked loudly over the sounds of the radio.

"Turn it down a little, Jenna," Alicia insisted. "The car's great, Mom. We love Gigi. Don't we, Jenna."

"She's good. But I still miss Drusilla," Jenna answered sadly. Alicia and Jenna always name their cars. Their first car was an ancient white Volvo they called Giles, after a character in the television series "Buffy the Vampire Slayer." The Honda Civic they just sold, after it finally gave up the ghost, was named Drusilla, who was also a character in the same series. Their current car had been my mom's car. It was a huge old green Pontiac with relatively low miles. They called her Gigi, short for GG or Green Goblin. It fit.

When we pulled into town, we found a large space for Gigi and went in search of a place to have lunch. We finally settled on Wildcat Willies. The décor was decidedly western and was reminiscent of the old Willie E. Coyote cartoons. Since the place is known for its barbecue, we ordered barbecue.

"Grandma! I love this place," Jenna said over lunch. "They have the

BEST sweet potato fries ever." I tried one of her fries and decided she was right.

"This really is a fun place, Mom," Alicia agreed. "Thanks for lunch."

"You're welcome, Boo." I said. Alicia Boo was my favorite nickname for Alicia when she was little. I have no idea how it got started. Sometimes I shortened it to just Boo, as I did today. Alicia still humors me and lets me use it on occasion. "Does anyone want dessert?" I asked.

"No, not me, Mom."

"Too full, Grandma."

"Ok. How about if I buy a fresh bumbleberry pie for later?"

"Yum! " Jenna said. "Sounds good, Grandma." After we bought the pie, we poked through the little art shops for a few hours, and I ended up purchasing a photograph of Zion's Canyon that Jenna picked out for me. Then we started back for St. George. By the time we got there, it was getting dark.

"What's next, ladies?" I asked.

"Would you like to drive over to the temple, maybe look at the Christmas lights, and walk around the Visitor's Center?" Alicia asked.

"I'd love that, Alicia. Yes. Thank you," I answered, knowing she was doing this in large part for me. "How about you, Jenna?"

"Ok. Sounds fun."

"Would you like to get dinner first," I asked.

"Let's eat later, Mom. We're closer to the temple than home." Alicia answered.

"I'll make chicken when we get home, Grandma," Jenna offered.

It was well past dinner time in my mind, but I didn't want to miss the opportunity to spend time together on the temple grounds. Then I remembered the bumble berry pie sitting next to me on the back seat. I quietly broke off a chunk of pie with my hands and pulled it from the tin under cover of darkness. I chewed noiselessly as luscious berries and still-warm pie filling swam happily in my mouth.

"Grandma!" Jenna exclaimed suddenly, turning around. "Are you eating our pie with your hands?"

I was caught. "Uh . . . yes, I suppose I am," I answered guiltily, my mouth still full of pie.

"Mom!" Alicia shouted from the front seat. And then she burst out laughing, as she turned around to see what I was doing. By this time, Jenna was laughing hysterically. "I can't believe you just ripped right into our pie without either a knife or fork," Alicia said. "Couldn't you wait?" And she laughed again.

"Apparently not," I answered, laughing along with them. Then I said, "Just remember, ladies. What happens in St. George stays in St. George." They both teased me mercilessly as we parked the car. And then they finally agreed to say nothing.

"Ok, Mom," Alicia said. "It'll be our little secret."

When we got inside the Visitor's Center, I asked the woman at the front desk where we could find the film, "Only a Stonecutter." Alicia had seen it before and wanted me to see it too. So did Jenna. The woman at the desk seemed somewhat amused as she turned us over to one of the sister missionaries. Perhaps she was just being friendly, I thought.

As we walked down the hall to the small viewing room, Alicia hissed quietly in my direction, "Mom . . . you might want to check your upper lip."

"What is it?" I asked, turning my head toward her.

"I think it's the pie," she said, trying hard not to laugh.

"Oh no," I said, reaching up and pulling off a purplish piece of sugary crust that sat anchored on my upper lip. So much for our little secret, I thought, relieved that I lived in California. At least I was presentable again by the time we sat down to watch the film.

We watched the tender story of a stone mason named John Rowe Moyle, who'd walked 22 miles to Salt Lake City for 20 years to chisel the granite stones for the Salt Lake Temple. He did this even after he lost one of his legs in an unrelated accident on his farm in Alpine. This same John Moyle had entered the Salt Lake Valley with the Ellsworth handcart company, along with my great-great-grandmother Selina Marshall. We were all in tears by the time the film ended.

I was touched that my girls were touched, and I wondered what it was that was keeping them from going back to church. Returning to my community of faith had brought me peace and made me happy. And I thought that maybe it would make Alicia and Jenna happy too. I didn't want to push them in any way, but maybe if I asked a curious question in a loving and caring way, it might be all right.

As we walked out into the cool night to see the multi-colored Christmas lights, Jenna walked on ahead of us. I put my arm around Alicia's shoulders and asked her the question that had been on my mind.

"Alicia, do you mind if I ask what's keeping you from going back to church?"

"I'd be ok to go to church, Mom. But I don't want to push Jenna," she answered. Made sense to me. So after we caught up with Jenna I asked her the same question.

"Jenna, do you mind if I ask what's keeping you from wanting to go to church?"

"It starts at 9:00 a.m., Grandma. I like to sleep in on Sundays." I smiled. She was 13 after all.

"So what if it started later, Jenna. Would you go then?" I asked.

"I guess so, yes. That would be ok."

"I think your meeting schedule might be changing in January," I said.

"What time will they start in January, Mom?" Jenna wondered.

"11:00," Alicia told her.

"I guess I'd go at 11:00," she decided.

"I'll go too, Mom, and take Jenna," Alicia said. The happy dance inside my head began in earnest. My girls had decided to start going to church again!

I didn't talk with Alicia the first few weeks in January, because she didn't have any minutes left on her phone. I really missed talking with her. The email exchanges and occasional texts were ok, but it wasn't the same as talking with her on the phone. She called me as soon as she could.

After we got caught up on Alicia's work and Jenna's school, I asked Alicia if she and Jenna had gone to church. And I held my breath waiting for her answer.

"I went by myself last week, Mom," Alicia said. "Jenna wouldn't go. She said she was too tired. When I walked out the door without her, she asked me if I were really going to go. I told her I was. And then I reminded her that a promise is a promise."

"Wow, Alicia," I said. "That sounds similar to something I would say."

"That's what I thought too, Mom," she laughed. "I sounded just like my mom." I was so proud of her for setting such a good example for Jenna, and I smiled happily. Although I knew that no daughter ever wants to sound just like her mom too often.

"Don't worry, Alicia," I said. "It's not a permanent condition." And we laughed again.

"Jenna went with me this Sunday, Mom. And she loved it. She found some girls she already knew. One of them is in her home room at school. Wednesday she went to Young Women's. It was spa night. She got her nails and hair done. She was so excited."

"And what about you, sweetie? How was it for you to go back to church?"

"I tried to avoid introducing myself in Sunday school and almost got away with it. But the lady sitting next to me pointed her hand down over my head and said, 'She's new. Ask her to introduce herself.'

"So I did. And then I told them I'd hoped not to have to introduce myself. They all laughed. One man came up to me after Sunday school and said, 'With a sense of humor such as that, Alicia, you'll fit right in here.' Then he walked me over to the Young Women's room, introduced his daughters to Jenna, and told them to take care of her."

"It sounds as if you and Jenna met nice people today, Alicia," I said.

"You're right, Mom, we did. And I think we both liked being there."

I was so relieved to hear that my girls had had a good experience at church. And I was filled with gratitude for ward members and Young Women leaders who had noticed Alicia and Jenna at church and welcomed them home.

# XXXVI

## Is There More?

I continued to look for divine guidance in my personal life. I was aware of the usual avenues of daily prayer and scripture study. And I had become an adherent of the idea that spiritual direction might come unexpectedly in a burst of light to my mind. But I was pretty sure that wasn't the usual method for me to receive ongoing spiritual assistance. I did know that leaving myself open to direction was key to receiving more direction. So I was particularly intrigued by a talk Richard G. Scott had given in General Conference. The title of his talk was: "To Acquire Spiritual Guidance."

I liked what Elder Scott had to say when I first heard his talk. About a month later, when I was seriously pondering crucial questions in my life, and wondering what to do next, I picked up the Ensign and started reading, looking for answers. I came across Elder Scott's talk again.

He spoke of receiving personal impressions that had come in response to his "prolonged, prayerful efforts to learn." He then said that as each impression came, he wrote it down. In the process of writing down his impressions, he was given "specific directions, instructions, and conditioned promises" that had "beneficially altered the course of [his] life."

He then prayed and reviewed what he thought he'd been taught. He was prompted to ask, "Is there more I should know?" That seemed as though it were a remarkable process to me. I particularly liked the part about writing down personal promptings, reviewing them in prayer, and then seeking to know if there was more. I'd never heard of anything similar to that before, and I wanted to try it for myself.

So I came up with my own short list of questions. I knelt down. I prayed humbly and sincerely. Then I got off my knees and recorded my promptings, as I understood them. I adjusted and refined what I'd written. I prayed again. And then I asked, "Is there more?" I followed that process for each one of my questions. And Elder Scott was right. In following these steps, I received some very direct and personal spiritual promptings. It was an incredible process.

There was something about writing down my impressions that led me to ask more questions and to receive more direction. The words seemed to be flowing from the pen in my hands and onto the page in front of me. I'd never had an experience similar to that before.

Just as I was about to conclude my prayers, I felt impressed to go back with what I thought was one smaller, and perhaps insignificant question, compared to the others. I'd been thinking about writing a book. I had two particular topics in mind, neither of which had been going anywhere for me at all. Maybe I simply wasn't capable of writing a book, I thought. But I took this one last question back to the Lord. As I prayed, the distinct impression that came to my mind was, "Call Soni. She knows what book you're supposed to write."

That answer was surprising to me; yet at the same time, it was not surprising at all. Soni knows all about writing and editing books. But she'd never been particularly receptive to any book ideas I'd run past her before. Maybe it was why I was still struggling to come up with a topic that would work.

I wasn't sure how Soni would react to my calling her, telling her that I felt impressed to write a book, and that I'd been given direction that she knew what book it was. While I knew Soni to be a deeply spiritual person, who had believed in my own spirituality when I didn't, I wasn't sure what her thoughts were on direct personal revelation.

What I did know was that I could talk with Soni about anything. And I had over the years. I had no fear of being either dismissed or judged. Or not heard or understood. That didn't mean that Soni wasn't sometimes frankly honest with me, or that I was not frankly honest with her. Sometimes one of us needed it. As in one day when she said to me, "Did you really just say that to Alex?" What it did mean was that whatever we said to each other was said out of a sense of respect and friendship.

Our conversations never ran as run-of-the mill conversations do.

They were always intensely interesting, at least to the two of us, and they didn't have a beginning, middle, or an end. By that I mean they didn't start with phrases such as, "How are you?" or, "What's new?" or, "Catch me up on what's happening." And they didn't end with phrases such as, "Well, it's good talking to you," or, "Let's talk again soon," or, "Call me."

Our conversations started in the middle of whatever topic was currently on one of our minds. And they ended because we simply ran out of time to talk. Which was not until several hours after the conversation began. Since my move away from Orange County 5 years ago, we neither saw nor talked with each other as often as we used to. But it didn't matter how often we talked. We always just picked up somewhere in the middle of wherever we'd left off.

But today, I was trying to figure out how to even begin this unusual conversation. What would she think? I needn't have worried about calling her. While I was debating on how best to phrase my question, Soni called me. As she began talking, and I stalled for time, she could tell that something was on my mind. "What is it, Susan?" she asked. So I said to myself, here it goes.

"I've been praying and writing today, Soni. One of the questions I prayed about was whether or not I should be writing a book."

"And what was your answer?" she asked.

"This may sound strange, but my answer was: 'Call Soni. She knows what book you're supposed to write.'" And then I paused.

In typical Soni fashion, she didn't miss a beat. "I don't think that sounds strange at all. I know exactly what book you're supposed to write."

"You *do?*" I asked, surprised. Even if she had some idea, I thought she might at least need some time to think about it. Maybe get back to me later.

"So, what is it?" I asked.

"I've been thinking about this for awhile, Susan. You need to share your story about going back to your faith. You could help others who are struggling with their faith, just as you were."

That possibility for a book hadn't crossed my mind. "Really?" I asked. "But Soni. I'm not sure I can even write a book. Let alone that one."

"Yes you can," she said. "I'll help you. I believe very strongly in this project. You can do this, Susan," she said. "In fact, you must do it."

"I must do it?" I repeated.

"Yes. This book will be important to others of your faith. It's your mission to write this book."

I had never heard Soni use the word mission about anyone or anything. She might use the word "beshert." But I'd never heard her use the word "mission." That word was straight out of my culture.

We talked for hours after that. We talked through thoughts, ideas, and a possible structure. We discussed a working title. "Do you really think I can do this, Soni?" I asked her again.

"Yes, Susan, I do," she reassured me.

As we began working together, she had to coach me over and over. When she read my first efforts, she said, "No, Susan. That's not what we're going for here." So I tried again. And again. Until she finally liked the outcome. I was glad she had a vision of where we were going. Because I certainly didn't. Not for months and months.

One day, after I'd been stuck for weeks, I called Soni again. I didn't know what to write about anymore or how to structure it. It all seemed very disjointed to me, and I didn't know how to make sense of it all. This was VERY hard work.

"Think of it as wandering around in the desert and looking for answers," she offered.

Didn't work for me. "That's not doing it," I said.

She tried again. "Think of it as one of those dot pictures. You won't know what it looks like until you're finished. Just write the dots. Don't worry about the structure for now. The structure will evolve. Just write the dots.

That made sense to me. I would write about each event that had been an important step in my journey and see where it took me. I'm typically an over-planner and not an evolver, so this was an entirely new process. But I found that I loved beginning a chapter and not knowing where it was going to end. Or even what it might ultimately be about. And my journey continued as I wrote. I thought about things I hadn't thought about in years. My eyes continued to open and my understanding grew.

Our day Soni said to me, "Our meeting 10 years ago has brought us to this point, Susan. This is where we're supposed to be. Here. Together. Working on this book." At first I was surprised at her words. But I couldn't disagree with what she said. This book is the end product of our close collaboration.

My purpose in sharing the very personal story I've told throughout these pages is a simple attempt to reach out to others who are either struggling with their own testimonies or the wavering testimonies of those they love. It's meant ultimately to be a message of hope.

More than anything, my story turned out to be a love story. A story filled with family members, friends, and home teachers who stood by me, loved me, and acted as true under-shepherds as I struggled for years to get my bearings and regain my faith. I give thanks daily that I finally found my way back home.

"Let us come before his presence with thanksgiving, and make a joyful noise unto him with psalms. For his is our God; and we are the people of his pasture; and the sheep of his hand." Psalm 95: 2 and 7

## EPILOGUE

# Being Home

*A*s this book goes to press, I've been home in the Church for about 3 years now. I can honestly say that I'm happier than I've ever been before. I have peace and real joy; I feel infused daily with my Heavenly Father's love. I feel good about who I am and what I'm doing. I have a quiet confidence that I've simply never felt before. I still regularly don't know how things will turn out, but I don't worry too much about it anymore. I've learned to manage the ambiguity life has to offer. I try to move forward daily with faith, trusting that the Lord is in charge. And I've discovered, much to my surprise, that my life works so much better now than when I was the one in charge. President Benson expressed it best when he said, "Men and women who turn their lives over to God will discover that He can make a lot more out of their lives than they can."

There was a time, even when I was at my most active in the Church, that I would not have understood what he meant by that. Now I do. I have learned that turning my life over to God's care and keeping can be nothing short of a miracle.

In March of 2011, my daughter-in-law Karry made the decision to join the Church. Four days before the baptism, Alex and Karry called me to go over the program. Alex had more news. "Bishop Hunter asked me to come and see him again tonight. We talked for about an hour. He wanted to know if I was ready to be ordained an elder."

That was huge. "What did you tell him?" I asked.

"I told him I was," Alex answered. "I know what I need to do. And I'm ready. The stake president agreed. So if the high councilors agree, I'm going to be ordained an elder just before Karry's baptism. And then I can also confirm Karry." Just when I thought things couldn't possibly get any better at this point in our collective lives, they simply did. Tears of joy ran down my face as I hung up the phone.

And so on the morning of March 26, Alex's dad, assisted by my 3 brothers and Bishop Hunter, ordained Alex an elder in the Melchizedek priesthood, handing down to Alex the authority to bless the life of his wife and someday his children. I watched my son stand a little taller as he hugged his priesthood brothers in the circle. They thumped each other fondly on the back, as men in the Church like to do. Alex seemed fully aware that he had assumed new responsibilities in his life. It came to me for the first time as I watched my son that holding the priesthood keeps men connected to their wives and children in ways they might not otherwise be. And I appreciated something I hadn't understood before.

Later that same morning, I watched my son raise his arm to the square and baptize his wife. Karry looked radiant in white as she expectantly placed her hand on Alex's arm and looked up into his face.

After they got dressed, Alex laid his hands on Karry's head and gave her the gift of the Holy Ghost and a blessing. I listened as Alex paused as he proceeded, obviously thinking deeply about just the right things to say to his wife. My reservoir of joy, which had spilled over weeks ago, burst its banks and flooded my heart. Both my children and my granddaughter were on their own journey home.

In the midst of all this joy, I realized, of course, that I didn't know what lay ahead for me and my children. There would no doubt be good days and bad days; both ups and downs. We are almost guaranteed moments of great joy and moments of deep sadness to come. But through it all, I trust that we will thrive, sustained by our deep and abiding trust and faith in God, surrounded by the people who love us.

# Acknowledgments

*I* express gratitude to those who have made this book a reality. I begin with my friend and editor, Soni Rice. I cannot say enough about her superb editing skills and her unfailing support of both me and my work.

I owe a great deal to the following people: Jeanne Jardine, for helping me find just the right title for my story; Richard G. Peterson for reading my manuscript and encouraging me to publish it; Susan Stevens, who picked me up when I needed it; the wonderful Australians for their feedback on my chapter, "Searching New Landscapes." (You know who you are.) My appreciation goes to Kristin Smith for being a thorough copy editor and to Kent Minson for his design work, both inside and out.

I would like to thank my family. My brothers Norm, Brent, and Dave, and my sisters-in-law Karla, Marcia, and Jaci, who not only read my manuscript and provided invaluable feedback, but who supported every step of my journey. To my children Alicia and Alex and my incredible granddaughter Jenna, who cheered me on from the very beginning. To my beautiful daughter-in-law Karry for her encouragement and early readings of my fledgling efforts; to my nephew Brent and nieces Emily and Annie for reading my words and understanding what I was trying to do. And last, but decidedly not least, to my mother Lucille Hatch Nielson, who not only prayed me home, but who thought everything I wrote was simply amazing, even when it wasn't.

Made in the USA
San Bernardino, CA
10 November 2012